本科规划教材

教育部中外语言交流合作中心2021年度《国际中文教育中文水平等级标准》
教学资源建设项目成果

相遇天府

中文视听说

Encountering Sichuan:
Chinese Video-watching,
Listening and Speaking

主　　编　李宏亮
副 主 编　陈泽丽　龙　梅
编写人员　黄　进　雷　岚　李书简
　　　　　刘玉梅　罗　阳　孙莉萍　许雪蕾
英文校对　[美] Nancy Westanmo–Head

电子科技大学出版社
University of Electronic Science and Technology of China Press

·成都·

图书在版编目(CIP)数据

相遇天府：中文视听说 / 李宏亮主编. — 成都：电子科技大学出版社，2023.11
ISBN 978-7-5647-9325-8

Ⅰ.①相… Ⅱ.①李… Ⅲ.①地方文化—研究—成都 ②汉语—听说教学—对外汉语教学—教材 Ⅳ.①G127.711②H195.4

中国版本图书馆CIP数据核字(2021)第252299号

相遇天府——中文视听说
XIANGYU TIANFU——ZHONGWEN SHI TING SHUO

李宏亮　主编

策划编辑	谢晓辉　魏祥林
责任编辑	于　兰
助理编辑	魏祥林
出版发行	电子科技大学出版社 成都市一环路东一段159号电子信息产业大厦九楼　邮编 610051
主　页	www.uestcp.com.cn
服务电话	028-83203399
邮购电话	028-83201495
印　刷	成都市金雅迪彩色印刷有限公司
成品尺寸	170mm×240mm
印　张	12.5
字　数	260千字
版　次	2023年11月第1版
印　次	2023年11月第1次印刷
书　号	ISBN 978-7-5647-9325-8
定　价	139.00元

版权所有　侵权必究

编写说明

一、适用对象

《相遇天府——中文视听说》适合中文水平为三级及以上的中文学习者学习使用，可作为选修课教材，也可作为对四川区域文化感兴趣的国际人士自学使用。

二、编写理念

近年来，供中文学习者使用的国别化教材越来越受到广大教师和学习者的重视和认同，其中一个重要的原因是此类教材切合了学习者的实际情况，更具针对性。然而，我们在教学中发现，国别化教材侧重于海外学习者的母语环境的具体情况，国内市面上常见的通用型教材也没有考虑到来华学习者所处的目标语环境的具体情况。中国是一个地理、人口大国，地域文化丰富，差异显著。21世纪以来，越来越多的国际人士到四川地区求学和工作，他们在学习和生活中迫切需要了解当地的文化。同时，目前市面上的教材以文字性材料为主，缺少生动的视听教材。

因此，在对学生和教师进行了充分的需求分析后，我们决定编写一部面向来川留学生的视听说教材，以帮助学习者更好地了解四川文化，提高跨文化交际能力。

本教材是一部视听说教材，以中文交际目标为导向，以四川文化内容为主线，把文化和语言教学密切结合。教材编写组招募、组织中外志愿者饰演不同的角色，按照话题录制为视频和音频，力求借助现代音像技术，使学习者了解和掌握四川区域文化，提高其语言交际能力。

三、教材体例

本教材以文化话题划分教学单元，一共十个单元，每个单元包含导入、生词和短语、视听说任务及练习、语法点注释、扩展活动以及文化小贴士等六个部分。各个部分环环相扣，循序渐进。每单元从引入相关话题入手，在让学习者学习生词和短语后，通过观看和听生动的语言文化材料，完成一系列练习活动，从而达到提高中文交际能力的目的。每个单元各部分内容的介绍如下所示：

（1）导入

从与本单元相关的问题入手，引起学习者的兴趣，引导学生初步了解本单元将要学习的话题。

（2）生词和短语

这一部分提供了本单元相关的词汇，放在每个视听任务之前，帮助学习者了解和掌握目标词语，扫清后续视听任务的词汇障碍。学习者可根据自身情况，有的进行重点掌握，有的作为一般性了解。

（3）任务及练习

这一部分是每个单元的重点，包括两个视频任务、两个音频任务。第一个视频为讲座形式，旨在以"教师"的角色为学习者提供本单元内容的介绍，使学习者在"导入"的基础上，对相关话题内容有一个总体的了解。另外的音频、视频任务从各个具体要素展开，是对此话题内容的进一步学习。学习者在完成视听任务后，再做相应的练习。这些练习活动形式多样、内容丰富，涵盖了语言技能的训练和文化内容的理解两个部分。教师和学生可根据实际需要，全部完成或选取一部分进行练习。

（4）语法点注释

每个单元的语法点注释涵盖了本单元出现的重要语法点，包含了语法结构和语用功能上的简要说明，并给出了一些例句，为教师的语言点教授和学生的语言点学习提供了帮助。

（5）拓展活动

该部分提供了一项课外语言文化实践活动，形式多样，如参观、调查、访谈等，目的是充分利用本地的文化资源，打通课堂内外，使学习者运用课堂所学知识，深入本土环境进一步了解和拓展本单元相关内容。

（6）文化小贴士

该部分对本单元相关的文化知识做了进一步的补充解释，目的在于引导学习者提高对相关文化概念的理性认知。教师可根据实际需要做出相应的讲解，感兴趣的学习者也可进一步查阅有关文献以达到较深入的认识和理解。

四、教材特色

（1）突出四川区域文化

本教材不是市面上常见的通用型教材，而是一部突出四川区域文化的区域型教材，从各个典型话题依次展开，使学生在视听练习中逐渐了解和认识常见的四川区域文化。前面九个单元聚焦于四川的高校、历史地理、气候交通、民俗、旅游资源、美食、川茶、生活方式等不同方面，立体地向学习者展示了绚丽多姿的"天府之国"。最后一个单元通过对四川文化与中国其他区域文化的比较，使学习者对四川区域文化有更加清晰的认识，也有利于学习者扩大视野，认识到中国文化的博大精深。

（2）文化内容安排有内在逻辑

教材的文化内容安排依据学习者在四川的学习、生活、成长过程，从学习者身边的学习环境入手，逐渐深入学习者生活中的各个方面，循序渐进，代入感强。整个教材像一部完整、精彩的影视剧。

（3）兼顾文化和语言要素

教材把文化知识和语言技能训练融为一体，不仅是对四川区域文化的介绍和展示，也是学习者学习和掌握相关语言表达的优秀语料。通过学习生词和短语、视听课文，以及完成练习活动，学习者的语言技能会在原有基础上进一步提高，而通过对各个单元文化内容的学习，学习者对四川的区域文化也将有整体性的了解和认识。

（4）趣味性、科学性和实用性结合

本教材采用视听说的形式，配有大量的视频、图片和音频资源，以及多样化的练习活动，使学习活动的趣味性大大增强。各个单元的语言点和文化内容是以《高等学校外国留学生汉语教学大纲（长期进修）》为依据，通过教材编委会多次讨论，结合学习者的实际生活和学习需求，遴选、整合而成，有利于学习者学以致用并解决他们在学习和生活中常见的语言文化问题。

五、人员分工

这部教材是编委会集体智慧的结晶，编写组的老师通过几十次线下、线上讨论，确定了教材名称、章节体例、文化和语言点、练习形式、照片选取等内容。每位编写者负责一个单元的具体内容和练习，之后又经过多次集体讨论、交叉修改，以及不断润色锤炼，最终成稿。李宏亮负责教材的构想设计以及第十单元的编写，雷岚负责第一单元，刘玉梅负责第二单元，陈泽丽负责第三单元，黄进负责第四单元，许雪蕾负责第五单元，龙梅负责第六单元，孙莉萍负责第七单元，罗阳负责第八单元，李书简负责第九单元。美国籍外教 Nancy Westanmo-Head 负责英语部分的校对。原航和牟柳负责教材视频、音频的录制工作。

六、使用建议

（1）本教材共十个单元，每单元建议四个学时，教师和学习者可根据需要选取。

第一单元至第五单元的视频和音频文件，请扫描下方二维码获取。

1~5 单元视频二维码　　　　　　1~5 单元音频二维码

第六单元至第十单元的视频和音频文件，请扫描下方二维码获取。

6~10 单元视频二维码　　　　　　6~10 单元音频二维码

（2）语法点注释力求简明扼要，教师可根据情况进行补充说明。

（3）拓展活动可作为课后作业使用，教师可补充一些文化和语言知识进行指导，并根据要求检查学习者的课外完成情况。

七、特别感谢

感谢电子科技大学国际教育学院原院长邱爱英教授、国际教育学院高世全院长、何琪蕾副院长和原副院长李晔对本教材的大力支持和指导。感谢教育部中外语言交流合作中心、电子科技大学教务处和国际教育学院对本教材立项和出版的大力支持和经费资助。

Introduction

Ⅰ. Target Users

Encountering Sichuan: Chinese Viewing, Listening and Speaking is edited for learners of Chinese at Level 3 and above, as an elective textbook, or for self-study of non-Chinese speakers interested in Sichuan culture.

Ⅱ. Editing Purpose

In recent years, nationalized teaching materials for Chinese language learners have become more and more popular among teachers and learners, one of the main reasons being that they are more relevant and tailored to the learners' realities. However, through our teaching process, we have found that country-specific materials focus more on the specific circumstances of overseas learners' native languages, and that the generic materials commonly available in China do not take into account the specific circumstances of the target language in which learners are in China. China is a large country in terms of geography and population, and has rich and significantly different regional cultures. In the 21st century, more and more people from other countries are coming to Sichuan to study and work, and they are in earnest need to understand the local culture in their studies and lives. Meanwhile, the textbooks currently on the market are mainly text-based materials and lack vivid audio-visual materials.

Therefore, after a thorough analysis of the needs of students and teachers, we have decided to develop an audio-visual textbook for international students in Sichuan to help them better understand the local culture and improve their intercultural communication skills.

This is an audio-visual textbook oriented towards the communicative objectives in Chinese, with the content of Sichuan culture as the major theme, closely integrating culture and language teaching. The editing team recruits Chinese and foreign volunteers to play different roles and record videos and audios according to respective topics, aiming to make use of modern audio-visual technology to enable learners to understand and master the regional culture of Sichuan as well as improve their communicative language skills.

Ⅲ. Textbook Format

The textbook is divided into ten units on cultural topics. Each unit contains six sections: Lead-in, Words & Expressions, audio-visual tasks and exercises, Grammar Notes, Extended Activities and Cultural Tips. All sections are interlinked and progress in a step-by-step manner. In each unit, learners start with the Lead-in questions, and after studying the new words and expressions, complete a series of practice activities through viewing and listening to vivid linguistic and cultural materials, with the aim of improving communicative competence in Chinese. Each section is shown as follows:

(1) Lead-in

Starting with questions related to the unit to arouse learners' interest and guide them to an initial understanding of the topic they will be studying in the unit.

(2) Words and Expressions

Providing words and expressions related to the unit, placed before each audiovisual task, to help learners understand and master the target words and to clear the vocabulary obstacles for subsequent audiovisual tasks. Learners may decide which of these words to be focused on, while which other to be acquainted with.

(3) Tasks and Exercises

Being the focus of each unit and consisting of two video tasks and two audio tasks. The first task is in the form of a teacher's lecture designed to provide learners with an introduction to the content of the unit and to give learners an overview of the topic. The other three audio and video tasks develop specific elements and provide further learning on the topic. After completing the audio-visual tasks, learners do exercises that are varied and informative, covering both language skill training and cultural understanding. Teachers and students may decide whether to complete all or select some of the exercises.

(4) Grammar Notes

Covering the important grammar points that appear in the unit, containing brief explanations of grammatical structures and pragmatic functions, and giving some example sentences to help teachers and students in teaching and learning the language points.

(5) Extended Activities

Providing an extra-curricular language and culture practice activity in various forms, such as visits, surveys and interviews, with the aim of making full use of local cultural resources, combining in and out of class learning, and enabling learners to apply what they have learnt in the classroom and delve into the local community to further understand and extend the relevant content of the unit.

(6) Cultural Tips

Offering further explanations of cultural knowledge related to this unit, with the aim of guiding learners to improve their rational understanding of relevant cultural concepts. Teachers can provide appropriate explanation, while interested learners can consult further relevant literature for a deeper understanding.

Ⅳ. Features

(1) Highlighting Sichuan Regional Culture

This textbook is not a generic textbook as is common in the market, but one that highlights the regional culture of Sichuan. Students are introduced to common Sichuan regional cultures through audio-visual exercises, starting with typical topics in turn. The first nine units focus on different aspects of Sichuan, including campus life, history and geography, climate and transport, folklore, tourism resources, cuisine, Sichuan tea and lifestyle, etc., showing learners a three-dimensional picture of the gorgeous "Land of Abundance". The last unit compares Sichuan culture with cultures of other regions of China, helping learners gain a clearer understanding of Sichuan culture as well as broaden their horizons and realize the profundity of Chinese culture.

(2) Arranging Cultural Content with Internal Logic

The cultural content of the textbook is arranged according to the learners' learning, living and growing up process in Sichuan, starting from the learning environment around them and gradually going into all aspects of life with a strong sense of immersion. The whole book is like a complete and exciting drama.

(3) Balancing Cultural and Linguistic Elements

The textbook integrates cultural knowledge and language skill training, and is not only an introduction to and a showcase of Sichuan regional culture, but also an excellent corpus for learning and mastering related expressions. By learning words and expressions, listening to the audios and watching the videos, and finishing practice activities, learners will build on their language skills, while through studying the cultural content of each unit, learners will gain a holistic understanding and appreciation of Sichuan regional culture.

(4) Integrating Fun, Science and Practicality

This textbook adopts an audio-visual format with a large number of videos, pictures and audios, as well as a variety of exercises, making the learning activities much more interesting. The language points and cultural content of each unit are based on the Syllabus for Teaching Chinese as a Foreign Language to Foreign Students in Higher Education, selected and integrated through many discussions by the textbook editorial committee who took into account the actual life and learning needs of learners, which is conducive to learners' application and solving common language and cultural problems in their study and life.

V. Task Division

The textbook is the result of the collective wisdom of the editorial committee. Members of the editing team discussed dozens of times offline and online to determine the title, the style of the all units, the cultural and linguistic points, the form of exercises, the selection of photographs and other aspects of the book. Each member was responsible for the script and exercises of one unit, which were then refined through numerous group discussions and cross-revisions. Li Hongliang was responsible for the design of the textbook and the writing of Unit 10, Lei Lan for Unit 1, Liu Yumei for Unit 2, Chen Zeli for Unit 3, Huang Jin for Unit 4, Xu Xuelei for Unit 5, Long Mei for Unit 6, Sun Liping for Unit 7, Luo Yang for Unit 8 and Li Shujian for Unit 9. Nancy Westanmo-Head, a native English teacher from America, was responsible for proofreading the content in English, while Yuan Hang and Mou Liu for the video and audio recording of the teaching materials.

VI. Suggestion

(1) This textbook consists of ten units, each of which is recommended to be completed in four credit hours, and can be selected by teachers and learners according to their needs.

Please scan the QR code below for the video and audio files from Unit 1 to 5.

Unit 1~5 video QR code   Unit 1~5 audio QR code

Please scan the QR code below for the video and audio files from Unit 6 to 10.

Unit 6~10 video QR code   Unit 6~10 audio QR code

(2) Grammar notes are brief, while teachers may provide additional clarification as appropriate.

(3) Extended activities can be used as after-school assignments where teachers may add some cultural and language knowledge for guidance and check learners' completion after class.

VII. Special Thanks

Special thanks go to Professor Di Aiying, former dean of the School of International Education of UESTC, Mr. Gao Shiquan, dean of the School of International Education of UESTC, Ms. He Qilei, vice dean of the School of International Education of UESTC, and Mr. Li Ye, former vice dean of the School of International Education of UESTC, who have provided support and guidance for this textbook. Deepest gratitude is expressed to the Center for Language Education and Cooperation, the Teaching Affairs Office and the School of International Education of UESTC for their approaval of the project and generous sponsorships of publishing the book.

主要人物介绍
Introduction to the Main Characters

刘老师：女，中国人，在成都高校工作多年，教留学生中文。
Prof. Liu: female, Chinese, a teacher of teaching Chinese to international learners at a university in Chengdu with rich work experience.

王　成：男，中国人，在成都读书，大学四年级。
Wang Cheng: male, Chinese, a fourth-year undergraduate in Chengdu.

赵丽川：女，中国人，在成都读书，大学二年级。
Zhao Lichuan: female, Chinese, a second-year undergraduate in Chengdu.

林一诺：男，加纳人，在成都留学七年，博士研究生一年级。
Lin Yinuo: male, Ganian, a first-year Phd student who has been studying in Chengdu for seven years.

何蓉蓉：女，巴基斯坦人，在成都留学五年，硕士研究生二年级。
He Rongrong: female, Pakistani, a second-year master's student, who has been studying in Chengdu for five years.

杜无羡：男，意大利人，在成都留学，大学三年级。
Du Wuxian: male, Italian, a third-year undergraduate in Chengdu.

丹　枫：女，缅甸人，在成都留学，大学一年级。
Dan Feng: female, Burmese, a first-year undergraduate in Chengdu.

词类简称表

1	名	名词	míngcí	noun
2	动	动词	dòngcí	verb
3	形	形容词	xíngróngcí	adjective
4	代	代词	dàicí	pronoun
5	数	数词	shùcí	numeral
6	量	量词	liàngcí	measure word
7	副	副词	fùcí	adverb
8	介	介词	jiècí	preposition
9	连	连词	liáncí	conjunction
10	助	助词	zhùcí	particle
		语气助词	yǔqì zhùcí	modal particle
		结构助词	jiégòu zhùcí	structural particle
		动态助词	dòngtài zhùcí	aspect particle
11	叹	叹词	tàncí	interjection
12	拟声	拟声词	nǐshēngcí	onomatopoeia
13	成	成语	chéngyǔ	idiom
14	短	短语	duǎnyǔ	phrase

目 录 Contents

第一单元　乐学成都
Unit 1　Campus Life ·· 1

第二单元　探源天府
Unit 2　Geography and History ·· 14

第三单元　宜居锦城
Unit 3　Climate and Transportation ·· 27

第四单元　蜀都访胜
Unit 4　Visits to Historical Sites ·· 38

第五单元　绚美四川
Unit 5　Travelling in Sichuan ·· 48

第六单元　蜀风艺海
Unit 6　Folklore and Featured Art in Sichuan ·· 63

第七单元　百味物语
Unit 7　Sichuan Cuisine ·· 73

第八单元　蓉城茶香
Unit 8　Sichuan Tea Culture ·· 87

第九单元　快享慢活
Unit 9　Contemporary Lifestyle in Chengdu ·········· 96

第十单元　多彩中国
Unit 10　Regional Differences in China ·········· 104

附录1：练习参考答案
Appendix 1　Key to the Exercises ·········· 114

附录2：词汇总表
Appendix 2　Vocabulary ·········· 123

附录3：音频、视频文本
Appendix 3　Audio and Video Scripts ·········· 152

第一单元　乐 学 成 都
Unit 1　Campus Life

导入（Lead-in）

你来中国学习多长时间了？你在哪所大学学习？你学习什么专业？可以介绍一下你的大学吗？

How long have you been studying in China? Which university do you study at? What is your major? Could you please introduce your university?

任务一（Task One）

看视频，完成练习 Watch the video and do the exercises.

生词和短语（New Words and Expressions）

1. 广场	guǎngchǎng	名	square, plaza
2. 摆放	bǎifàng	动	to put in order
3. 旗杆	qígān	名	flagpole, flag post
4. 通道	tōngdào	名	passageway
5. 优雅	yōuyǎ	形	elegant, graceful
6. 可爱	kě'ài	形	cute
7. 陪伴	péibàn	动	to accompany

001

续表
Continued

8. 追求	zhuīqiú	动	to pursue, aspire
9. 梦想	mèngxiǎng	名	dream
10. 舒适	shūshì	形	comfortable
11. 丰富	fēngfù	形	abundant, rich
12. 整齐	zhěngqí	形	neat, in good order
13. 温暖	wēnnuǎn	形	warm
14. 大型	dàxíng	形	large, large-scale
15. 美丽	měilì	形	beautiful
16. 湿地公园	shīdì gōngyuán	短	wetland park
17. 绿树成荫	lǜshù chéngyīn	短	green trees make a pleasant shade
18. 开启	kāiqǐ	动	to open, to unlock

专有名词（Proper Names）

1. 银杏大道	Yínxìng Dàdào	Ginkgo Avenue
2. 东湖	Dōnghú	East Lake
3. 西湖	Xīhú	West Lake
4. 校友林	Xiàoyǒu Lín	Alumni Grove

（一）看视频，在地图上标注你听到的地方 Watch the video and mark the places mentioned in the following map.

a. 南门 (nán mén)　b. 主楼 (zhǔ lóu)　c. 主楼广场 (zhǔ lóu guǎng chǎng)　d. 银杏大道 (yín xìng dà dào)　e. 东湖 (dōng hú)

f. 校友林 (xiào yǒu lín)　g. 西湖 (xī hú)　h. 教学楼 (jiào xué lóu)　i. 图书馆 (tú shū guǎn)　j. 时间广场 (shí jiān guǎng chǎng)

k. 食堂 (shí táng)　l. 宿舍楼 (sù shè lóu)　m. 篮球场 (lán qiú chǎng)　n. 足球场 (zú qiú chǎng)　o. 网球场 (wǎng qiú chǎng)

大学校园地图（Map of a University）

（二）根据视频内容，判断正误 Decide whether the following statements are true or false according the video.

(　　) 1. 主楼在学校的西门。

(　　) 2. 校园里有两个湖——东湖和西湖。

(　　) 3. 学生们喜欢去湖边运动、早读和玩儿。

(　　) 4. 图书馆和时间广场在教学楼的对面。

(　　) 5. 校园的西边有运动场，比如，篮球场、足球场和网球场。

相遇天府 —— 中文视听说
Encountering Sichuan: Chinese Video-watching, Listening and Speaking

（三）根据视频内容填空 Fill in the blanks according to the video.

1. 我们从南门进入校园，首先看到的是_____的主楼。
2. 学校的食堂_____舒适，菜品丰富。
3. 食堂的后边是一座座整齐的_____。
4. 西门附近有一条美丽的小河，河边是湿地_____。
5. 这里，_____桃红李白，_____绿树成荫，_____银杏金黄，冬天梅花飘香。

任务二（Task Two）

听录音，完成练习 Listen to the recording and do the exercises.

杜无羡和以前的中文老师打电话聊天，聊在中国的学习和生活。

Du Wuxian is calling his previous Chinese teacher, chatting about his study and life in China.

体育馆（A Stadium）　　　冬日校园（Campus in Winter）

生词和短语（New Words and Expressions）

1. 生活	shēnghuó	名、动	life; to live
2. 联系	liánxì	动	to contact
3. 习惯	xíguàn	动	to be accustomed to
4. 差不多	chà·buduō*	副	almost

*一般轻读、间或重读的字，注音时在该字的拼音前加上圆点。

续表
Continued

5. 除了	chúle	介	besides, except
6. 困难	kùn·nan	形	difficult
7. 一般	yìbān	副	commonly, usually
8. 健身	jiànshēn	动	to go to the gym, to work out
9. 充实	chōngshí	形	rich, plentiful, full
10. 专业课	zhuānyèkè	名	professional course, major course
11. 选修课	xuǎnxiūkè	名	elective course, optional course
12. 有关	yǒuguān	形	related to
13. 感兴趣	gǎnxìngqù	短	to be interested in
14. 朋友圈	péngyouquān	名	moments (usu. in WeChat)
15. 组织	zǔzhī	动	to organize

（一）根据录音内容，判断正误 Decide whether the following statements are true or false according to the recording.

（　　）1. 杜无美和文老师有一年没联系了。
（　　）2. 杜无美每天上午和下午都有课。
（　　）3. 杜无美在学校只学习汉语。
（　　）4. 杜无美对中国文化很感兴趣。
（　　）5. 杜无美很喜欢旅游，他在中国去了很多地方。

（二）根据录音内容，选择正确答案 Choose the correct answers according to the recording.

（　　）1. 杜无美早上几点开始上课？
　　　　A. 八点半　　　　B. 九点
　　　　C. 九点半　　　　D. 十点
（　　）2. 杜无美什么时候起床困难？
　　　　A. 生病的时候　　B. 没课的时候
　　　　C. 天气冷的时候　D. 周末的时候

（　　）3. 下午的课是从几点到几点？
A. 一点到三点半　　　　B. 两点到四点
C. 两点半到四点多　　　D. 三点到五点

（　　）4. 下课以后，杜无羡常常做什么？
A. 运动健身　　　　　　B. 去图书馆
C. 和中国朋友聊天　　　D. 旅游

（　　）5. 文老师是怎么知道杜无羡在中国去了很多地方的？
A. 是杜无羡告诉老师的
B. 是杜无羡的朋友告诉老师的
C. 是老师在杜无羡的朋友圈里看到的
D. 是老师自己猜的

（三）讨论 Discussion

1. 你在学校学习什么课程？你们有选修课吗？
2. 你喜欢旅游吗？你去过什么地方？你们学校会组织旅游活动吗？
3. 你认为旅游对学习汉语有帮助吗？

任务三（Task Three）

观看视频，完成练习 Watch the video and do the exercises.

丹枫和杜无羡在逛校园。
Dan Feng and Du Wuxian are strolling around the campus.

银杏大道（Yinxing Avenue）

生词和短语（New Words and Expressions）

1. 天鹅	tiān'é	名	swan
2. 金灿灿	jīncàncàn	形	golden
3. 举办	jǔbàn	动	to run, to conduct, to hold
4. 美景	měijǐng	名	beautiful scenery
5. 传统	chuántǒng	名	tradition
6. 谜语	míyǔ	名	riddle
7. 摄影展	shèyǐngzhǎn	名	photographic exhibition
8. 美食展	měishízhǎn	名	food show
9. 热闹	rè·nao	形	lively, joyful
10. 灿烂	cànlàn	形	bright, magnificent
11. 金黄	jīnhuáng	形	golden yellow
12. 确实	quèshí	副	indeed

专有名词（Proper Names）

| 银杏节 | Yínxìng Jié | Ginkgo Festival |

（一）根据视频内容，回答问题 Answer the following questions according to the video.

1. 杜无美喜欢早上在湖边做什么？

2. 为什么十一月是学校最漂亮的时候？

3. 什么是银杏节？

4. 银杏节期间有什么活动？

5. 为什么他们笑女孩子喜欢"美丽冻人"？"美丽冻人"和"美丽动人"有什么区别？

6. 他们打算去哪儿喝咖啡？

（二）口语练习 Speaking Practice

说一说你们学校什么时候最漂亮，有没有特别的节日。节日的时候，学校会举行特别的活动吗？

When is your school's most beautiful time? Is there a special festival of your school? During the festival, will the school hold some related activities?

任务四（Task Four）

听录音，完成练习 Listen to the recording and do the exercises.

在生日聚会上，丹枫、杜无羡和何蓉蓉一起聊天。
Dan Feng, Du Wuxian and He Rongrong are chatting at a birthday party.

生词和短语（New Words and Expressions）

1. 百听不厌	bǎitīng-búyàn	成	worth hearing a hundred times
2. 茉莉	mò·lì	名	jasmine
3. 花茶	huāchá	名	flower tea
4. 资料	zīliào	名	material
5. 实验室	shíyànshì	名	laboratory
6. 导师	dǎoshī	名	supervisor
7. 放松	fàngsōng	动	to relax
8. 美食街	měishíjiē	名	food street

续表
Continued

9.便利	biànlì	形	convenient
10.购物中心	gòuwù zhōngxīn	短	shopping mall
11.中心	zhōngxīn	名	centre
12.逛街	guàng jiē	动	to go shopping, to stroll on the street
13.娱乐	yúlè	名	entertainment

专有名词（Proper Names）

1.康定情歌	Kāngdìng Qínggē	Kangding Love Song, name of a song
2.茉莉花	Mò·lì Huā	Jasmine Flower, name of a song

（一）根据录音内容，选择正确答案 Choose the correct answers according to the recording.

（　　）1.今天谁过生日？
　　A.杜无美　　B.丹枫　　C.何蓉蓉　　D.丹枫的朋友
（　　）2.丹枫喜欢哪两首歌？
　　A.《茉莉花》　B.《成都》　C.《康定情歌》　D.《朋友》
（　　）3.研究生不常做什么？
　　A.去图书馆看书查资料　　B.去实验室工作
　　C.跟导师见面　　D.找兼职工作
（　　）4.杜无美觉得校园里的生活怎么样？
　　A.很方便　　B.很休闲　　C.很便宜　　D.很无聊
（　　）5.何蓉蓉周末喜欢去哪儿？
　　A.校内的美食街　　B.校园里的咖啡馆
　　C.学校附近的购物中心　　D.图书馆

（二）讨论 Discussion

1.你喜欢听汉语歌吗？你听过哪些汉语歌？
2.周末的时候你怎么休息放松？

3.你觉得校园生活怎么样?

语法点注释（Grammar Notes）

1.主楼广场上摆放着鲜花。

　旗杆上挂着五星红旗。

　图书馆和时间广场，从早到晚陪伴着每一个学子。

　那个女孩还穿着裙子呢!

动词后面加上动态助词"着"表示动作或状态的持续。

A verb adding the dynamic auxiliary "着" expresses the processing of an action or the continuation of a state.

表示动作的持续时，动词所表示的动作是可持续性的。"动词+着"常与"正在""正""在"等词连用。例如：

To indicate the processing of an action, the verb should express a continuous action and usually used together with "正在""正""在" etc. For example：

①课间休息同学们正聊着天，突然老师进来了。

②外面正下着大雨呢，等一会儿再去食堂吧。

表示状态的持续。

To indicate the continuation of a state.

③教室里的空调开着。

④今天的讲座太精彩了，教室里的学生可真多，有的一直站着。

本结构常常用于表达人物的穿着打扮或表示事物的存在。

This structure is often used to express the dressing of people or existence of things.

⑤学生们头上戴着学士帽，手里拿着毕业证，站在教学楼前照相。

⑥每一张课桌上都放着一台电脑。

2.不过，下午一般只有两节课，从两点半上到四点多。

"不过"是连词，常常用于句首，表示对上文所表达意思的转折。

"不过" is a conjunction, often used at the beginning of a sentence to indicate the transition of the meaning in the context.

①A：我们中午一起去吃饭吧，我请客。

　B：好啊!不过不用你请客，咱们"AA制"。

②我们这学期的汉语课不多。不过，听说下学期有中国文化课，我很感兴趣。

③今天的气温很低，不过，天气好，阳光灿烂，是拍照的好时候！

④虽然每天学习都挺忙，不过，我每周都会找时间放松一下，跟朋友出去吃吃饭、聊聊天。

扩展活动（Extended Activities）

（一）听歌曲学汉语 Listen to songs and learn Chinese

你喜欢听中文歌曲吗？你最喜欢的中文歌曲是什么？你听过《I Love the City》和《成都》这两首歌曲吗？你知道这两首歌的歌词吗？

请你和同学互相交流分享，说一说对成都这座城市的感受。

Do you like listening to Chinese songs? What is your favorite Chinese song? Have you ever listened to "I Love the City" and "Chengdu" these two songs? Do you know the lyrics?

Please communicate and share your impression towards Chengdu this city with your classmates.

（二）欢迎新同学 Welcome new comers

新学年开始了，学校又迎来了一批新同学。作为高年级学生，请向新同学介绍大学的基本情况，比如，校园介绍，留学生活动，学习要求，住宿条件，餐饮服务，签证申请，周边环境，等等。

A new semester begins. Another group of new students have come to the university. As a senior student, please give a vivid introduction to these new comers. For example, campus tour, international students' activity, academic requirements, accommodation, catering service, visa application and school surroundings.

📝 文化小贴士（Cultural Tips）

成都知名的高等院校

1. 四川大学始建于1896年，是一所著名的研究型综合大学。学科门类齐全，校园风景秀丽。其华西医学中心源于华西协和大学，后者是西南地区最早的西式大学，也是中国最早的医学综合性大学，其建筑风格独特，特别是华西坝融中国古典园林和西方宫廷花园于一体。

2. 电子科技大学是一所以电子信息科学技术为核心的多科性研究型大学，是国内电子信息领域高新技术的源头、创新人才的基地。学校以工为主，理、工、管、文、医协调发展。"求实求真、大气大为"为电子科技大学的校训。

3. 西南交通大学是中国第一所工程教育高等学府，拥有交通运输工程、桥梁与隧道工程等国家重点学科，建有轨道交通国家实验室（筹）、牵引动力国家重点实验室等。

4. 西南财经大学有着独特的金融行业背景和出色的金融学科优势，是国家金融、经济、管理等部门高水平人才培养的重要基地，被誉为"中国金融人才库"。

5. 西南民族大学专注于民族高等教育，招收56个民族的在校全日制学生。学校拥有极富特色的民族博物馆和全国高校中规模最大的藏学文献馆、世界上规模最大的彝学文献馆。

6. 四川师范大学是四川省属重点大学，是四川省举办本科师范教育最早的院校。

这些高校各具特色，各有所长，在新时代的今天，以崭新的姿态、开放的胸襟，迎接着来自海内外的莘莘学子。

Well-known Colleges and Universities in Chengdu

1. Founded in 1896, Sichuan University is a famous research-oriented comprehensive university. It has a wide range of disciplines and enjoys beautiful campus scenery. Its West China Medical Center originated from West China Union University, the first western style one in Southwest China, and also the earliest comprehensive medical university in China. Its architectural style is unique, especially the Huaxi Ba Campus which integrates Chinese classical gardens and western court ones.

2. University of Electronic Science and Technology of China is a key multidisciplinary research university with electronic information sci-tech as its nucleus, engineering as its major field and features the harmonious integration of science, engineering, management and liberal arts. It is China's cradle for the national electronic industry and also the base of innovative talents. It takes "to seek facts and truth, to be noble and ambitious" as the university motto in the pursuit of excellence.

3. Southwest Jiaotong University is the first institution of higher engineering education in China. It is known as "the cradle of railway engineers in China". It covers such national key disciplines as transportation engineering, bridge and tunnel engineering, and has established the National Laboratory for Rail Transit (preparatory), the National Key Laboratory for Traction Power, etc.

4. Southwest University of Finance and Economics has a unique financial industry background and outstanding financial discipline advantages. It is an important base for high-level talents training in national finance, economy, management and other departments, and is known as the "China Financial Talent Pool".

5. Southwest Minzu University focuses on higher ethnic education and enrolls full-time students from 56 ethnic groups. The university has a distinctive ethnic museum, the largest Tibetan literature museum among national colleges and universities, and the largest Yi literature museum in the world.

6. Sichuan Normal University is a key university in Sichuan Province. It was the pioneering provincial university to hold undergraduate normal education and has developed into a cradle of teachers for Sichuan and China at large.

In short, each of these universities has its own characteristics and strengths. In this new era, they are stretching their arms to welcome students from home and abroad with a new glamour and an open mind.

第二单元 探源天府
Unit 2　Geography and History

导入（Lead-in）

你知道成都这个城市名字的故事吗？你听说过哪些和成都有关的故事呢？

Do you know anything about the name of Chengdu? Have you ever heard of any stories about Chengdu?

任务一（Task One）

看视频，完成练习 Watch the video and do the exercises.

成都天府国际金融中心双塔
（Twin Towers in Chengdu）

成都合江亭
（Hejiang Pavilion in Chengdu）

Unit 2　Geography and History

生词和短语（New Words and Expressions）

1.	西南	xīnán	名	southwest
2.	盆地	péndì	名	basin
3.	平原	píngyuán	名	plain
4.	省会	shěnghuì	名	provincial capital
5.	地区	dìqū	名	area, region
6.	发达	fādá	形	developed, advanced
7.	地势	dìshì	名	terrain, topography
8.	平坦	píngtǎn	形	flat, smooth
9.	河流	héliú	名	river
10.	农业	nóngyè	名	agriculture, farming
11.	物产	wùchǎn	名	product
12.	养	yǎng	动	to raise, to grow, to keep
13.	织	zhī	动	to weave, to knit
14.	蚕	cán	名	silk worm
15.	锦	jǐn	名	brocade
16.	历史悠久	lìshǐ yōujiǔ	短	to have a long history
17.	历史	lìshǐ	名	history
18.	悠久	yōujiǔ	形	time-honored, long-standing
19.	古	gǔ	形	ancient, age-old
20.	文化	wénhuà	名	culture
21.	居住	jūzhù	动	to live, to dwell
22.	留下	liúxià	短	to leave behind
23.	名胜古迹	míngshèng gǔjì	短	scenic spots and historic places
24.	都城	dūchéng	名	capital
25.	场所	chǎngsuǒ	名	site, place
26.	政治	zhèngzhì	名	politics

续表
Continued

27. 军事	jūnshì	名	military
28. 人物	rénwù	名	personage, person, figure
29. 使用	shǐyòng	动	to use, to employ
30. 街道	jiēdào	名	street, road
31. 名称	míngchēng	名	name (of an object or organization)
32. 大街小巷	dàjiē-xiǎoxiàng	成	high streets and back lanes

专有名词（Proper Names）

1. 成华区	Chénghuá Qū	Chenghua District, a district of Chengdu City
2. 锦江区	Jǐnjiāng Qū	Jinjiang District, a district of Chengdu City
3. 武侯区	Wǔhóu Qū	Wuhou District, a district of Chengdu City
4. 高新区	Gāoxīn Qū	Shortform of Hi-tech Industrial Development Zone, a district of Chengdu City
5. 岷江	Mínjiāng	Minjiang River
6. 府河	Fǔhé	Fuhe River
7. 南河	Nánhé	Nanhe River
8. 都江堰水利工程	Dūjiāngyàn Shuǐlì Gōngchéng	the Dujiangyan Water Conservancy Project
9. 蜀	Shǔ	an ancient state name of Sichuan area in history, another name for Sichuan Province
10. 宽窄巷子	Kuānzhǎi Xiàng·zi	the Wide and Narrow Alleys, ancient streets in Chengdu

（一）根据视频内容，判断正误 Decide whether the following statements are true or false according to the video.

（　）1. 成都位于中国西南部。
（　）2. 春熙路在成华区。
（　）3. 成都的"母亲河"是"锦江"。

（　　）4. 成都也可以叫作"锦城"或者"锦官城"。
（　　）5. "成都"这个名字已经用了2000多年了。
（　　）6. 成都是世界上最早用纸币的地方。
（　　）7. 诸葛亮是1700多年以前三国时期的人物。

（二）根据视频内容填空 Fill in the blanks according to the video.

1. 成都在中国_____，位于四川盆地西部、成都平原_____。
2. 成都平原地势平坦，有很多_____的河流。
3. 成都也是一座国家历史文化_____城，是古蜀文化_____的重要地方。_____多年前人们就_____在这里居住生活了。
4. 成都市的金沙遗址，就是_____3000年前古蜀时期人们的活动场所。
5. 成都还是世界上最早使用纸币的地方，那时候的纸币_____"交子"。
6. 成都还有很多的街道名称都_____成都的历史和人们的生活_____。

任务二（Task Two）

听录音，完成练习 Listen to the recording and do the exercises.

新学期开始了，丹枫和赵丽川在教学楼前聊天。

At the beginning of the new semester, Dan Feng meets Zhao Lichuan in front of the teaching building and they have a chat.

街道（A Street）　　　　　　　芙蓉花（Hibiscus）

生词和短语（New Words and Expressions）

1. 看起来	kànqǐlái	短	seemingly
2. 休闲	xiūxián	形	leisurely
3. 越来越	yuèláiyuè	短	increasingly
4. 堵车	dǔ chē	动	to get stuck in a traffic jam
5. 轻松	qīngsōng	形	relaxed
6. 心情	xīnqíng	名	mood, state of mind
7. 建设	jiànshè	动	to build, to develop
8. 宜居城市	yíjū chéngshì	短	livable city
9. 断	duàn	动	to stop, to cut off
10. 生机勃勃	shēngjī-bóbó	成	vivifying
11. 芙蓉花	fúrónghuā	名	hibiscus

（一）根据录音内容，判断正误 Decide whether the following statements are true or false according to the recording.

(   ) 1. 从机场到学校，丹枫坐了一个多小时的出租车。
(   ) 2. 学校在成都的东南边。
(   ) 3. 以前成都的房子有点儿贵。
(   ) 4. 一到周末成都就会堵车。
(   ) 5. 成都也叫"蓉城"。
(   ) 6. 丹枫已经见过芙蓉花了。

（二）根据录音内容填空 Fill in the blanks according to the recording.

丹枫昨天才到成都。从_____到学校，她坐了_____一个小时的出租车。来学校的路上，她看见路上有_____，人也_____，她觉得成都不_____。中国的同学告诉她因为成都_____的发展，城市＿＿＿＿＿，人们的生活也不＿＿＿＿＿了。而且成都常常＿＿＿＿＿。不过，她觉得成都的路两边有很多花和树，＿＿＿＿＿的时候，看看它们，心情可能会好＿＿＿＿＿。中国同学还告诉她成都也叫＿＿＿＿＿，所以＿＿＿＿＿都能看见芙蓉花。可是她还＿＿＿＿＿芙蓉花。中国同学说如果＿＿＿＿＿就带她去看芙蓉花。

（三）口语练习 Speaking Practice

你的家乡有具有代表性的花吗？如果有，请介绍一下；如果没有，请介绍一下你最喜欢的一种花（包括它的名字、颜色、什么时候开花和它的历史等）。

Is there a flower which represents your hometown? If so, please introduce it; if not, please introduce a flower which you like best, including its name, color, blooming time and history, etc.

任务三（Task Three）

看视频，完成练习 Watch the video and do the exercises.

留学生何蓉蓉、夏涛和中国学生赵丽川一起参观天府广场。

Chinese student Zhao Lichuan takes international students He Rongrong and Xia Tao to visit Tianfu Square.

成都天府广场（Chengdu Tianfu Square）　　成都金沙遗址（Chengdu Jinsha Relics）

相遇天府 ——中文视听说

Encountering Sichuan: Chinese Video-watching, Listening and Speaking

生词和短语（New Words and Expressions）

1. 地理	dìlǐ	名	geography
2. 天然	tiānrán	形	natural
3. 府库	fǔkù	名	government treasury
4. 旱	hàn	名	drought
5. 涝	lào	名	flood, waterlogging
6. 粮食	liáng·shi	名	food, foodstuff
7. 充裕	chōngyù	形	abundant, plentiful
8. 战争	zhànzhēng	名	war, warfare
9. 富足	fùzú	形	abundant, plentiful
10. 安定	āndìng	形	stable, settled
11. 雕塑	diāosù	名	sculpture
12. 图案	tú'àn	名	pattern, design
13. 阳光	yángguāng	名	sunlight
14. 发现	fāxiàn	动	to discover
15. 象征	xiàngzhēng	名、动	symbol; to symbolize
16. 表达	biǎodá	动	to convey, to express
17. 崇拜	chóngbài	名、动	worship; to worship
18. 的确	díquè	副	indeed
19. 听起来	tīngqǐlái	短	to sound
20. 改天	gǎitiān	副	some other day

专有名词（Proper Names）

金沙遗址	Jīnshā Yízhǐ	Jinsha Relics, a historical relic of ancient Shu culture

（一）根据视频内容，选择正确答案 Choose the correct answers according to the video.

(　　) 1. 天安门广场在_____。
  A. 北京 B. 上海 C. 成都 D. 广州

Unit 2　Geography and History

（　　）2. "国"在"天府之国"里的意思是_____。
　　A. 国家　　B. 中国　　　　C. 地方　　　　D. 家乡

（　　）3. "太阳神鸟"图案中十二道阳光象征_____。
　　A. 十二年　　　　　　B. 十二个月
　　C. 十二个国家　　　　D. 十二个国王

（　　）4. "太阳神鸟"的图案是在_____发现的。
　　A. 都江堰　　　　　　B. 天府广场下面
　　C. 金沙遗址　　　　　D. 人民广场下面

（　　）5. 金沙遗址离天府广场大概_____公里。
　　A. 1　　　B. 4　　　C. 5　　　D. 6

（二）根据视频内容，回答问题 Answer the following questions according to the video.

1. 成都平原为什么叫"天府之国"？

2. "太阳神鸟"的图案表达了什么意思？

任务四（Task Four）

听对话，完成练习 Listen to the dialogue and do the exercises.

中国学生王成和留学生林一诺、丁思尧在买完东西后进行交谈。
Chinese student Wang Cheng chats with international students Lin Yinuo and Ding Siyao after shopping in a store.

成都九眼桥夜景
（Chengdu Jiuyan Bridge at night）

成都洗面桥街
（Chengdu Ximianqiao Street）

相遇天府 ——中文视听说
Encountering Sichuan: Chinese Video-watching, Listening and Speaking

生词和短语（New Words and Expressions）

1. 付	fù	动	to pay (money)
2. 现金	xiànjīn	名	cash
3. 声调	shēngdiào	名	tones (of Chinese characters)
4. 纸	zhǐ	名	paper
5. 假	jiǎ	形	fake
6. 幽默	yōumò	形	humorous
7. 纪念	jìniàn	动	to commemorate, to remember
8. 发明	fāmíng	名	invention
9. 深厚	shēnhòu	形	profound
10. 皇帝	huángdì	名	emperor
11. 将军	jiāngjūn	名	general
12. 据说	jùshuō	动	it is said that ...
13. 失败	shībài	名、动	failure; to fail
14. 修	xiū	动	to build, to construct
15. 庙	miào	名	temple, memorial temple

专有名词（Proper Names）

1. 交子大道	Jiāozǐ Dàdào	Jiaozi Avenue
2. 九眼桥	Jiǔyǎn Qiáo	Jiuyan Bridge
3. 合江亭	Héjiāng Tíng	Hejiang Pavilion
4. 洗面桥	Xǐmiàn Qiáo	Ximian Bridge
5. 刘备	Liú Bèi	Liu Bei (161–223), the first emperor of the Kingdom of Shu from the Three Kingdoms era of China
6. 关羽	Guān Yǔ	Guan Yu (?–220), a general serving under the warlord Liu Bei

（一）三人一组表演这个对话 Three students work together to act out the conversation.

（二）小组讨论 Group Discussion

在中国越来越多的人用手机付钱,你们觉得这样有什么好处？有什么问题？

四个人一组进行讨论,然后选一个人做课堂报告。请将讨论的关键词写在下面的表格中。

In China, more and more people use smartphones to pay bills. What advantages and disadvantages do you think it will bring to people's life?

Four students work together to have a discussion and then choose a representative to do the report. Write down the key words in the following table.

用手机付钱(pay with smartphones)	
好处（advantages）	
问题（disadvantages）	

语法点注释（Grammar Notes）

1. 房子比以前贵多了。

"比"可以用来比较两个人或者两件事情在性状或者程度上的差别,其否定形式为"没有(没)……"。

The preposition "比" can be used to indicate the differences in property or degree of two items and its negative is expressed by"没有(没)".

①他比我高。　　　　　　　　我没有他高。
②四川省比成都市大。　　　　成都市没有四川省大。
③北京的冬天比成都的冬天冷。　成都的冬天没有北京的冬天冷。

2. 现在城区越来越大，人口也越来越多。

"越来越"可以用来表示某人或某事在某方面的程度是随时间的推移发生变化的。

"越来越" may be used to show that a certain person or thing changes in a certain aspect as the time goes on.

①成都市的交通越来越方便了。
②孩子们越来越喜欢学习了。
③成都市的绿地和公园越来越多，越来越漂亮。

扩展活动（Extended Activities）

天府故事会 （Sharing Old Stories of Chengdu）

课后邀请一位中国朋友和你一起去了解成都一条街道名字的故事，并制作视频，然后完成下面的表格，最后在课堂上分享有关这条街道的故事。

After class, invite a Chinese friend to help you to know the story of a street in Chengdu and make a video. Then finish the following form and share what you've known about the street in class.

Streets you can visit：

| 琴台路 | 暑袜街 | 草堂路 | 浣花南路 | 华兴街 | 宽巷子 |
| 蜀汉路 | 春熙路 | 锦里古街 | 盐道街 | | |

成都的一个街道(a street in Chengdu)	
名字(name)	
在哪儿(where)	
名字跟什么有关 (what's the name related to)	
历史(history)	

第二单元 探源天府
Unit 2　Geography and History

📝 文化小贴士（Cultural Tips）

1. 都江堰水利工程（Dujiangyan Water Conservancy Project）

都江堰水利工程（Dujiangyan Water Conservancy Project）
（田捷砚　摄　Photographed by Tian Jieyan）

都江堰水利工程已经有2000多年的历史了。这个工程并不破坏自然环境，而是利用自然资源为人类服务，从而变害为利，使人、地、水和谐（héxié, harmoniouly)共处。它是世界上唯一留存下来的最古老的生态工程。

The Dujiangyan Water Conservancy Project was built more than 2,000 years ago. Its design does not pose a threat to natural environment; instead, it fully capitalizes on the natural resources to benefit human beings. In this way, it turns floods into a boon for the local people, thus achieving the harmony among people, land and water. It is the only "ecological project" that is still exists and functions today in the world.

2. 金沙遗址（Jinsha Relics）

"太阳神鸟"金饰雕塑
（Sculpture of the Sun and Immortal Birds Gold Ornament）

025

金沙遗址是2001年2月在成都市区发现的,是距今3200～2600年的长江上游古代文明中心——古蜀王国——的都邑(dūyì, capital)。金沙遗址和三星堆都是四川省重要的考古发现(kǎogǔ fāxiàn, archeological discovery)。

Jinsha Relics was unearthed in February, 2001 in Chengdu. It was the capital of the ancient Shu Kingdom, a civilization center about 2,600 years to 3,200 years ago. Jinsha Relics and Sanxingdui Site are both important archaeological discoveries in Sichuan Province.

第三单元 宜居锦城
Unit 3 Climate and Transportation

导入（Lead-in）

你觉得成都的气候怎么样？成都的交通呢？

What do you think about Chengdu's climate? And what about its transportation?

任务一（Task One）

看视频，完成练习 Watch the video and do the exercises.

生词和短语（New Words and Expressions）

1. 宜居	yíjū	形	livable, suitable for living
2. 气候	qìhòu	名	climate, weather
3. 湿润	shīrùn	形	wet, humid
4. 皮肤	pífū	名	skin
5. 国际	guójì	名、形	world; international
6. 枢纽	shūniǔ	名	hub
7. 航班	hángbān	名	flight
8. 单车	dānchē	名	bike
9. 应用程序	yìngyòng chéngxù	短	application

相遇天府——中文视听说
Encountering Sichuan: Chinese Video-watching, Listening and Speaking

专有名词 (Proper Names)

| 1. 双流国际机场 | Shuāngliú Guójì Jīchǎng | Shuangliu International Airport |
| 2. 天府通 | Tiānfǔtōng | Tianfutong Card, Tianfutong App |

（一）根据视频内容，判断正误 Decide whether the following statements are true or false according to the video.

（　）1. 成都春秋两季不冷不热。
（　）2. 成都常常晚上下雨，第二天下午才停。
（　）3. 春秋两季去成都玩最好。
（　）4. 成都有三个客运火车站，分别在成都市区的东边、西边和北边。
（　）5. 在成都，你用天府通公交卡坐公交车，票价打八折。

（二）根据视频内容填空 Fill in the blanks according to the video.

1. 成都是一座很_____的城市，_____很好。
2. 成都空气比较_____，对皮肤很好。
3. 双流国际机场是西南地区的_____，有飞往中国_____的_____，也有飞往亚洲、非洲、欧洲、美洲和大洋洲的航班。
4. 成都市区公共交通很发达，_____、_____、_____班次都比较多，又快又方便。
5. 你可以用手机下载天府通应用程序，_____扫码乘车。

任务二 (Task Two)

听录音，完成练习 Listen to the recording and do the exercises.

赵丽川和林一诺在学校门口的有轨电车站等车，去机场接新生丹枫。
Zhao Lichuan and Lin Yinuo are waiting for the trolley at the trolley station next to the school gate. They are going to pick up Dan Feng, the freshman, at the airport.

Unit 3　Climate and Transportation

有轨电车站（A Trolley Station）

生词和短语（New Words and Expressions）

1. 有轨电车	yǒuguǐ diànchē	短	tramcar, trolley
2. 通车	tōngchē	动	to be open to traffic
3. 投币	tóu bì	短	to insert coins
4. 终点站	zhōngdiǎnzhàn	名	destination
5. 赶	gǎn	动	to hurry through
6. 体验	tǐyàn	名、动	experience; to experience
7. 电子显示屏	diànzǐ xiǎnshìpíng	短	electronic screen
8. 先进	xiānjìn	形	advanced

专有名词（Proper Names）

1. 成都西站	Chéngdūxī Zhàn	Chengdu West Station
2. 文化宫站	Wénhuàgōng Zhàn	Cultural Palace Station
3. 太平园站	Tàipíngyuán Zhàn	Taipingyuan Station

（一）根据录音内容，选择正确答案 Choose the correct answers according to the recording.

（　）1. 有轨电车什么时候通车？
　　　　A. 上个月　　B. 去年　　C. 上星期　　D. 下星期

（　　）2. 林一诺坐过有轨电车吗？

　　　A. 没坐过　　　B. 坐过　　　C. 不知道　　　D. 不确定

（　　）3. 乘客不能_____乘坐有轨电车。

　　　A. 刷公交卡　　B. 刷脸　　　C. 投币　　　　D. 付费

（　　）4. 林一诺和赵丽川坐有轨电车，要在哪个站下？

　　　A. 文化宫站　　　　　　　B. 太平园站

　　　C. 成都西站　　　　　　　D. 双流机场

（　　）5. 下面哪个说法不正确？

　　　A. 乘成都地铁10号线可以到机场。

　　　B. 有轨电车站有电车线路图，也有电子显示屏。

　　　C. 电子显示屏上只用中文显示时间和车次。

　　　D. 林一诺没带公交卡。

（二）根据录音内容，回答问题 Answer the following questions according to the recording.

1. 林一诺和赵丽川打算怎么去机场？

2. 电子显示屏是什么样子的？你觉得车站上的电子显示屏怎么样？

任务三（Task Three）

看视频，完成练习 Watch the video and do the exercises.

在春熙路地铁站，王成等丹枫和林一诺一起去杜甫草堂等景点玩。

At the Chunxi Road Metro Station, Wang Cheng is waiting for Dan Feng and Lin Yinuo. They are going to visit Dufu Thatched Cottage and other places together.

春熙路地铁站（Chunxi Road Metro Station）

生词和短语（New Words and Expressions）

| 1. 景点 | jǐngdiǎn | 名 | scenic spot |
| 2. 人山人海 | rénshān-rénhǎi | 成 | a sea of people, crowded conditions |

专有名词（Proper Names）

| 1. 春熙路 | Chūnxī Lù | Chunxi Road, a prosperous commercial street in Chengdu City |
| 2. 杜甫 | Dù Fǔ | Du Fu, a famous poet in the Tang dynasty |

（一）根据视频内容，判断正误 Decide whether the following statements are true or false according to the video.

(　　) 1. 市中心很热闹。

(　　) 2. 春熙路人很多。

(　　) 3. 地铁每五分钟就有一班。

(　　) 4. 昨天晚上下雨了，但今天早晨天晴了。

(　　) 5. 他们打算坐景区直通车去玩。

（二）根据视频内容，回答问题 Answer the following questions according to the recording.

1. 春熙路怎么样？
_____

2. 成都地铁怎么样？
_____

3. 成都春天的天气有什么特点？
_____

（三）角色扮演 Role-play

根据对话内容，三个学生一组，分角色表演这个对话。

Based on the conversation, work in a group of three students and role-play this conversation.

任务四（Task Four）

听录音，完成练习 Listen to the recording and do the exercises.

赵丽川和林一诺在双流机场第二航站楼到达出口接丹枫。

Zhao Lichuan and Lin Yinuo are waiting to pick up Dan Feng at the Arrival Hall of T2, Shuangliu International Airport.

Unit 3　Climate and Transportation

双流国际机场（Shuangliu International Airport）

双流国际机场到达厅（Arrival Hall of Shuangliu International Airport）

生词和短语（New Words and Expressions）

| 1. 航站楼 | hángzhànlóu | 名 | terminal |
| 2. 牌子 | páizi | 名 | sign |

专有名词（Proper Names）

| 天府国际机场 | Tiānfǔ Guójì Jīchǎng | Tianfu International Airport |

033

相遇天府
——中文视听说
Encountering Sichuan: Chinese Video-watching, Listening and Speaking

（一）根据录音内容，判断正误 Decide whether the following statements are true or false according to the recording.

（　）1. 丹枫的航班是到T2航站楼。
（　）2. 赵丽川和丹枫是第一次见面。
（　）3. 丹枫觉得中国的机场又大又漂亮。
（　）4. 成都有两个机场。
（　）5. 他们坐公交车回学校。

（二）根据录音内容，回答问题 Answer the following questions according to the recording.

1. 丹枫是怎么从她的国家来到成都的？

_____

2. 林一诺和赵丽川是怎么认出丹枫的？

_____

📝 语法点注释（Grammar Notes）

1. 我还没有坐过有轨电车呢，想试试。

动词后加上动态助词"过"，一般用来表示过去有过的经历，这些动作、行为没有持续到现在。在动词前边加"没（有）"，表示否定。

A verb followed by the aspect particle "过" usually indicates a past experience action which hasn't lasted to the present. In the negative form, "没（有）" is put before the verb.

①你坐过有轨电车吗？
②我昨天上网查过了。
③我还没（有）坐过呢。

2.这么多地铁出口，我们从哪个口出去呢？

"这么"加在形容词前面，表示程度高。在"这么"前边加"没(有)"表示否定。

" 这么 " can be put before an adjective to indicate "high degree". In the negative form, "没(有)" is used before "这么".

①这么多人，我们回去的时候会不会等很久才能上车啊？

②中国的机场都这么大、这么漂亮吗？

③地铁票没（有）这么贵。

扩展活动（Extended Activities）

乘车方案

周末,你和你的同学都有出行计划。有的要去成都东站接朋友,有的要去天府广场买东西,还有的要去杜甫草堂玩儿。

请查看成都交通地图,制定出从学校出发,分别去到成都东站、天府广场和杜甫草堂的乘车方案,画出示意图并讲解。全班分为三组,每组完成去一个目的地的乘车方案。请每组提出至少两个乘车方案,并综合考虑乘车时间、换乘次数、步行距离远近及费用等因素,确定最优方案。

Transport Plans

On weekends, you and your classmates all plan to go out in Chengdu. Some are going to pick up their friends at Chengdu East Railway Station, some are going shopping at Tianfu Square, and some are going to visit Du Fu Thatched Cottage.

Please check the transport map of Chengdu and work out the transport plan from the school to Chengdu East Railway Station, to Tianfu Square and to Du Fu Thatched Cottage respectively. Then draw a schematic diagram and explain it in class. The class is divided into three groups, and each group completes a transport plan of going to one destination. Each group is expected to propose at least two transport plans, and to determine the optimal plan by considering comprehensively the travel time, number of transfers, walking distance and fare, etc.

相遇天府——中文视听说
Encountering Sichuan: Chinese Video-watching, Listening and Speaking

根据提示，写出要点 Write down the key points according to the questions.

	我的家乡 (my hometown)	成都 (Chengdu)
气候怎么样？ (How is the climate like?) 四季的天气怎么样？ (How is the weather in the four seasons like?)		
交通方便吗？ (Is the transportation convenient?) 人们一般乘什么交通工具出行？ (What kind of the transportation means do people usually take?)		

口头报告 Oral Presentation

你家乡的气候和交通怎么样？请根据以下要点准备一个两分钟的课堂口头报告。

What is the climate of your hometown like? And how about the transportation? Make a 2-minute talk about your hometown's climate and transportation in class. Your presentation is expected to include:

你的家乡在哪儿？
你的家乡气候怎么样？
你的家乡交通方便吗？
……

Unit 3　Climate and Transportation

📝 文化小贴士（Cultural Tips）

杜甫和《春夜喜雨》

杜甫（712—770年）是唐代著名诗人，被称为"诗圣"。他住在成都时，写了一首关于成都春天的诗。

春夜喜雨

好雨知时节，当春乃发生。
随风潜入夜，润物细无声。
野径云俱黑，江船火独明。
晓看红湿处，花重锦官城。

Du Fu and *Happy Rain on a Spring Night*

Du Fu (712–770), a great Chinese poet in the Tang dynasty, is called "Sage of Poetry" for his renowned masterpieces. He wrote a poem about Chengdu's spring when he lived in Chengdu.

Timely Rain on a Spring Night

As if knowing too well what is good timing,
Spring rain comes at the best time of spring.
Riding the wind and creeping into the night,
It nourishes all things with its silent drizzling.
Pathswind through complete dark in the wilderness,
A lone boat on the river is the only spot of light.
At dawn red blossoms are seen blooming in wetness,
Clusters after clusters across the Brocade City within sight.

译者吴永强

Translated by
Wu Yongqiang

第四单元 蜀都访胜
Unit 4　Visits to Historical Sites

导入（Lead-in）

关于成都的历史遗迹和传统文化,你了解多少？印象如何？

Regarding the historical sites and traditional culture in Chengdu, how much do you know? What's your impression?

任务一（Task One）

看视频，完成练习 Watch the video and do the exercises.

关羽(Guan Yu)　　　　　玉佛(Jade Buddha)

Unit 4　Visits to Historical Sites

生词和短语（New Words and Expressions）

1. 繁华	fánhuá	形	prosperous, booming
2. 拥有	yōngyǒu	动	to possess, to have
3. 独特	dútè	形	unique
4. 寺庙	sìmiào	名	temple
5. 景观	jǐngguān	名	scenery, landscape
6. 区域	qūyù	名	region
7. 特色	tèsè	名	feature
8. 道教	Dàojiào	名	Taoism, Daoism
9. 宫观	gōngguàn	名	(Taoist) temple and palace
10. 建筑	jiànzhù	名	architecture
11. 修建	xiūjiàn	动	to build, to construct
12. 绘画	huìhuà	名	painting
13. 宗教	zōngjiào	名	religion
14. 民俗	mínsú	名	folk customs
15. 佛教	Fójiào	名	Buddhism
16. 重修	chóngxiū	动	to rebuild
17. 寺院	sìyuàn	名	(Buddhist) monastery
18. 禅宗	chánzōng	名	the Zen sect (of Buddhism)
19. 丞相	chéngxiàng	名	premier (of ancient China)
20. 中华	Zhōnghuá	名	(formal and literary) China
21. 符号	fúhào	名	symbol, mark
22. 大熊猫	dàxióngmāo	名	giant panda
23. 国宝	guóbǎo	名	national treasure
24. 基地	jīdì	名	base
25. 竹子	zhúzi	名	bamboo

相遇天府 —— 中文视听说
Encountering Sichuan: Chinese Video-watching, Listening and Speaking

专有名词（Proper Names）

1. 诸葛亮	Zhūgě Liàng	Zhuge Liang (181–234), premier of the Shu state
2. 青羊宫	Qīngyáng Gōng	the Qingyang Temple
3. 武侯祠	Wǔhóu Cí	the Wuhou Shrine, Marquis Wu's Shrine
4. 文殊院	Wénshū Yuàn	the Wenshu Monastery

（一）根据视频内容，选择正确答案 Choose the correct answers according to the video.

（　）1. 青羊宫是什么宗教场所？
   A. 道教　　　B. 佛教　　　C. 禅宗　　　D. 儒家

（　）2. 如果有人想了解成都的佛教文化，你建议他去哪里？
   A. 武侯祠　　B. 青羊宫　　C. 文殊院　　D. 熊猫基地

（　）3. 武侯祠里纪念的"忠诚和智慧的象征"是谁？
   A. 刘备　　　B. 诸葛亮　　C. 蜀国　　　D. 三国时期

（　）4. 三国时期离现在大概有多少年？
   A. 2000多年　B. 1400年　　C. 1700年　　D. 300年

（　）5. 视频中提到的一种全世界都喜欢的动物是什么？
   A. 狗　　　　B. 猫　　　　C. 大熊猫　　D. 牛

（二）口头报告 Oral Presentation

总结一下本视频介绍了什么历史遗迹和传统文化。

Summarize orally the major historical sites and related traditional culture mentioned in the video.

任务二（Task Two）

听录音，完成练习 Listen to the recording and do the exercises.

赵丽川、杜无羡和王成聊成都名胜古迹。

第四单元 蜀都访胜
Unit 4　Visits to Historical Sites

Zhao Lichuan, Du Wuxian and Wang Cheng are talking about cultural and historical sites in Chengdu.

青羊宫（The Qingyang Temple）

生词和短语（New Words and Expressions）

1. 楹联	yínglián	名	couplet written on scrolls and hung on pillars
2. 表演	biǎoyǎn	动	to perform
3. 接触	jiēchù	动	to get in touch
4. 碰头	pèng tóu	动	to meet
5. 武术	wǔshù	名	martial art
6. 高人	gāorén	名	person of superior ability or accomplishment
7. 定	dìng	动	to decide

（一）根据录音内容，回答问题 Answer the following questions according to the recording.

1. 杜无羡以前去过青羊宫吗？

2. 在青羊宫可以体验哪些传统艺术？

3. 从他们那里到青羊宫，要走很远的路吗？交通方便不方便？

4. 杜无美想在手机上查什么？查到了吗？为什么？

5. 请说一说他们去青羊宫的详细计划。

（二）讨论 Discussion

道教主张自然的生活，你怎么理解"自然"？关于道教，你还知道什么？
Taoism advocates a natural way of living. How do you understand it? What else do you know about Taoism?

任务三（Task Three）

看视频，完成练习 Watch a video and do the exercises.

赵丽川、丁思尧和王成一起去参观文殊院。
Zhao Lichuan, Ding Siyao and Wang Cheng are visiting the Wenshu Monastery.

文殊院（The Wenshu Monastery）

Unit 4　Visits to Historical Sites

生词和短语（New Words and Expressions）

1. 环境	huánjìng	名	environment
2. 清静	qīngjìng	形	quiet and sobering
3. 噪声	zàoshēng	名	noise
4. 匆忙	cōngmáng	形	hasty
5. 脚步	jiǎobù	名	footstep
6. 目的	mùdì	名	objective, purpose
7. 冥想	míngxiǎng	动	to meditate
8. 打坐	dǎ zuò	动	to sit in meditation
9. 静坐	jìngzuò	动	to sit quietly and meditate
10. 尊	zūn	量	indicating a unit or a piece of sculpture
11. 菩萨	púsà	名	Bodhisattva (second only to Buddha)
12. 塑像	sùxiàng	名	sculpted statue
13. 算了	suànle	动	to forget it, to just stop at that, to let it go at that
14. 难为	nán·wei	动	to make it difficult, to be taxing
15. 复杂	fùzá	形	complicated
16. 翻译	fānyì	动	to translate
17. 弄懂	nòngdǒng	动	to understand
18. 典型	diǎnxíng	形	typical
19. 风格	fēnggé	名	style
20. 塑造	sùzào	动	to mould
21. 玉佛	yùfó	名	jade Buddha
22. 展览	zhǎnlǎn	动	to exhibit

专有名词（Proper Names）

缅甸	Miǎndiàn	Myanmar

（一）根据视频内容，回答问题 Answer the following questions according to the video.

1. 文殊院的环境怎么样？为什么？

2. 王成说，很多人去文殊院的目的是什么？

3. 文殊院在中国禅宗中的地位怎么样？

4. 文殊院现在的建筑主要是大约多少年前重修的？

5. 文殊院里面有一个展览室，是做什么用的？

（二）根据视频内容填空 Fill in the blanks according to the video.

1. 文殊院的_____真不错，一进来就感觉很_____。
2. 好像不少西方人现在也喜欢禅了。他们对冥想很_____。
3. 放慢_____，放松_____，体验_____。很多人来文殊院，就是为了这个目的。
4. 不要紧，虽然我弄不懂，但是至少可以看看这里的_____、_____、_____什么的。
5. 文殊院现在的建筑是大约三百年前_____的，是典型的清代四川西部风格。

任务四（Task Four）

听录音，完成练习 Listen to the recording and do the exercises.

王成、赵丽川和杜无羡聊武侯祠和熊猫基地。

Unit 4　Visits to Historical Sites

Wang Cheng, Zhao Lichuan and Du Wuxian are talking about the Wuhou Shrine and the Panda Base.

武侯祠（The Wuhou Shrine）

生词和短语（New Words and Expressions）

1. 政治家	zhèngzhìjiā	名	statesman
2. 既……又……	jì... yòu...	连	both...and...
3. 工艺品	gōngyìpǐn	名	handicraft, artifact
4. 推荐	tuījiàn	动	to recommend

（一）根据录音内容，判断正误 Decide whether the following statements are true or false according to the recording.

(　　) 1. 成都的名胜古迹，杜无羡几乎都去过了。
(　　) 2. 诸葛亮是三国时期的政治家。
(　　) 3. 刘备是蜀国的皇帝。
(　　) 4. 诸葛亮是忠诚和智慧的象征。
(　　) 5. 熊猫喜欢爬树，吃竹子。

（二）角色扮演 Role-play

和同学分角色表演这个对话，可以适当修改原文。

Work in groups and act out this dialogue with your peers. Use your own words if you like.

语法点注释（Grammar Notes）

1. 但是至少可以看看这里的建筑、雕塑、书法什么的。

口语中，常常在举例完毕时加上助词"什么的"，表示举例的行为到此为止。该助词是非正式用语，其含义与英语的"etc""and so on""or the like"非常相似。

The particle "什么的" is often used in oral Chinese at the end of the examples or cases cited, indicating the end of the exemplification. This particle is semantically close to "etc" "and so on" and "or the like".

①金钱并不能买到所有的东西，比如青春、友谊、健康什么的。

2. 我还是第一次从你这儿听到。

英语语法中的"v.+from+sb"结构使用频繁。但对应的中文翻译，常常变成"从+sb+这里/这儿/那里/那儿+v."结构。

In English grammar, the structure of "v. + from + sb" is frequently used. The corresponding Chinese translation, however, favors the structure of "从+sb+这里/这儿/那里/那儿+v.".

试比较下列例句。

Compare the following examples.

①我们可以从老子那里学到很多东西。
②他从朋友那儿借了50元钱。
③别想从我这儿得到任何消息！保密！

请注意上述例句中的"这里/这儿/那里/那儿"等词语是必须使用的，尽管英语结构中并无对应词语。

Please remember such words as "这里/这儿/那里/那儿" are compulsory in this case and context, although their equivalents are omitted and only the pronouns are used in these corresponding English structures.

扩展活动（Extended Activities）

有空去青羊宫、文殊院、武侯祠、宽窄巷子、成都熊猫基地等现场参观体验，然后在课堂上给大家做一个参观报告。

Pay visits, at your convenience, to the Qingyang Temple, the Wenshu Monastery, the Wuhou Shrine, the Wide and Narrow Alleys and the Chengdu Panda Base to have live experiences. And then do a presentation in class.

文化小贴士（Cultural Tips）

道教、佛教、儒家思想是中国传统文化中的三大部分。道教的自然无为、回归天真，佛教的谈心论性和人人可以成佛的平等思想，以及儒家的仁、义、礼、智、信、忠、孝等思想，对中国社会影响很大。了解了这些文化背景以后，在参观道教的青羊宫、佛教的文殊院、儒家的武侯祠时，就可能会有更深的理解和体验。诸葛亮作为政治家，是儒家价值的代表，实际上成了儒家文化符号。很多中国人并不是严格意义的信徒，他们的精神世界是道、佛、儒的自由选择组合。

Taoism, Buddhism and Confucianism are the three pillars of traditional Chinese culture. Taoism advocates "naturalness", "inaction", and "return to primordial simplicity". Buddhism features "equality" as in the proposition that every one can be a Buddha, and prominently elaborates the concepts of "mind" and "Buddha nature". Confucianism holds such tenets as "humanity", "righteousness", "propriety", "wisdom", "credibility", "loyalty", "filial piety", etc. These values are every influential in Chinese society, and the knowledge of them enables visitors to better understand the Qingyang Temple, the Wenshu Monastery and the Wuhou Shrine. The statesman Zhuge Liang of the Wuhou Shrine has become a symbol of Confucian values. Many Chinese are not strict followers of these thoughts while their spiritual world is a combination of all these three elements based on free, individualistic and practical selection.

第五单元 绚美四川
Unit 5　Travelling in Sichuan

导入（Lead-in）

看图片，说说你觉得这些地方怎么样。看看你能用哪些词来描述图片上的地方。

Look at the following pictures and tell the class how you feel about the places. Use as many words as possible to describe them.

Unit 5　Travelling in Sichuan

任务一（Task One）

看视频，完成练习 Watch the video and do the exercises.

生词和短语（New Words and Expressions）

1. 四面八方	sìmiàn-bāfāng	成	all directions
2. 优美	yōuměi	形	graceful, beautiful
3. 水利工程	shuǐlì gōngchéng	短	water conservancy project, irrigation works, irrigation system
4. 稍	shāo	副	slightly, a bit
5. 选择	xuǎnzé	动	to choose, to select
6. 迷人	mírén	形	fascinating, charming
7. 峡谷	xiágǔ	名	gorge, canyon
8. 冰川	bīngchuān	名	glacier
9. 神奇	shénqí	形	magical, miraculous, mystical
10. 流连忘返	liúlián-wàngfǎn	成	to enjoy oneself so much as to forget to go back
11. 传说	chuánshuō	名	legend, tale

专有名词（Proper Names）

1. 青城山	Qīngchéng Shān	Mount Qingcheng
2. 乐山	Lèshān	Leshan City, a city in Sichuan Province
3. 峨眉山	Éméi Shān	Mount Emei
4. 乐山大佛	Lèshān Dàfó	Leshan Giant Buddha
5. 九寨沟	Jiǔzhài Gōu	Jiuzhai Valley Scenic and Historic Interest Area
6. 黄龙	Huánglóng	Huanglong Scenic and Historic Interest Area
7. 自贡恐龙博物馆	Zìgòng Kǒnglóng Bówùguǎn	Zigong Dinosaur Museum
8. 蜀南竹海	Shǔnán Zhúhǎi	Southern Sichuan Bamboo Sea
9. 兴文石林	Xīngwén Shílín	Xingwen Stone Forest

（一）根据视频内容，选择正确答案 Choose the correct answers according to the video.

（　　）1. 都江堰是一个有千年历史的_____。
A. 交通要道　　　B. 书院　　　C. 水利工程　　　D. 寺庙

（　　）2. _____是"佛教名山"。
A. 青城山　　　B. 峨眉山　　　C. 乐山　　　D. 黄山

（　　）3. _____在川南地区。
A. 九寨沟　　　B. 黄龙　　　C. 都江堰　　　D. 蜀南竹海

（　　）4. 想看雪山、草原，就要去_____旅行。
A. 川东　　　B. 川南　　　C. 川西　　　D. 川北

（二）根据视频内容，选择正确的词填空 Choose the correct words to fill in the blanks according to the video.

九寨沟　黄龙　都江堰　青城山　乐山　峨眉山　川南　川西

来成都的游客一般先在市区游玩，然后出发去其他地方。大多数第一次来成都的游客都会去附近的_____和_____；他们也可以去离成都稍远一点儿的_____和_____；如果还想走得更远一些，游客们可以去风景迷人的_____和_____；如果有三四天时间，游客们可以去_____旅行；如果特别喜欢自然风光，就一定要去_____旅行了。

💡 任务二（Task Two）

听录音，完成练习 Listen to the recording and do the exercises.

杜无羡、王成和赵丽川聊他们的"五一"旅游计划。
Du Wuxian, Wang Cheng and Zhao Lichuan are talking about their travel plan for the May Day holiday.

Unit 5　Travelling in Sichuan

生词和短语（New Words and Expressions）

1. 简直	jiǎnzhí	副	simply, just, virtually
2. 说法	shuōfǎ	名	way of saying
3. 想象	xiǎngxiàng	动	to imagine
4. 雕刻	diāokè	动	to carve
5. 了不起	liǎo·buqǐ	形	amazing, terrific, extraordinary
6. 天下	tiānxià	名	land under heaven
7. 秀	xiù	形	beautiful, elegant, graceful
8. 拜佛	bài fó	动	to worship Buddha
9. 幸运	xìngyùn	形	lucky
10. 光环	guānghuán	名	a circle of light, halo
11. 运气	yùn·qi	名	luck
12. 零食	língshí	名	snack

（一）根据录音内容，判断正误 Decide whether the following statements are true or false according to the recording.

（　）1. 乐山大佛有差不多十二层楼那么高。

（　）2. 乐山大佛的一只脚上可以坐两百多个人。

（　）3. 乐山大佛是1300多年前建造的。

（　）4. 峨眉山有"峨眉天下秀"的美名，那里风景很漂亮。

（　）5. 峨眉山是中国的佛教名山，山上有很多道观。

（　）6. 峨眉山的山顶叫"金顶"。

（　）7. 运气好的话，在峨眉山顶上可以看到佛光。

（　）8. 峨眉山上有很多大熊猫。

（二）根据录音内容填空 Fill in the blanks according to the recording.

从乐山、峨眉山旅游回来之后，杜无羡写了一篇日记。请用你在对话中听到的词将日记补充完整。

After the trip to Leshan and Mount Emei, Du Wuxian wrote a diary. Please complete his diary with the words you hear in the conversation.

这个"五一"假期，我和王成、赵丽川一起去了乐山、峨眉山旅游。我们先去了乐山，看到了"_____"。它像山一样_____。一千多年以前，人们把一座山雕刻成一_____佛，真是太_____了！我们还爬了峨眉山。我去山上的寺庙里_____，希望我们能有好_____。没想到，我们真的非常_____，在山顶上看到了"云海"和"佛光"。"佛光"简直太_____了！另外，峨眉山上的_____也很有趣，它们吃了很多我准备的_____。

峨眉山金顶塑像（Statue on the Top of Mount Emei）

Unit 5　Travelling in Sichuan

乐山大佛（Leshan Giant Buddha）

任务三（Task Three）

看视频，完成练习 Watch the video and do the exercises.

杜无羡、王成和赵丽川聊暑假去哪儿旅游。

Du Wuxian, Wang Cheng and Zhao Lichuan are talking about where to travel during the coming summer holiday.

生词和短语（New Words and Expressions）

1. 暑假	shǔjià	名	summer holiday
2. 归来	guīlái	动	to return
3. 瀑布	pùbù	名	waterfall
4. 五颜六色	wǔyán-liùsè	成	colorful
5. 童话	tónghuà	名	fairy tale

053

续表
Continued

6. 当地人	dāngdì rén	短	local people
7. 叫法	jiàofǎ	名	way of naming a thing
8. 等不及	děng·bují	动	can't wait
9. 巨龙	jùlóng	名	giant dragon
10. 海拔	hǎibá	名	altitude
11. 高原反应	gāoyuán fǎnyìng	短	altitude sickness
12. 高原	gāoyuán	名	plateau
13. 神话	shénhuà	名	mythology, myth
14. 神仙	shénxiān	名	immortal, fairy
15. 五彩斑斓	wǔcǎi-bānlán	成	multicolored and bright-colored
16. 到底	dàodǐ	副	on earth
17. 遗憾	yíhàn	动	to regret

专有名词（Proper Names）

1. 阿坝州	Ābà Zhōu	Aba Tibetan and Qiang Autonomous Prefecture
2. 世界自然遗产	Shìjiè Zìrán Yíchǎn	World Natural Heritage
3. 国家5A级旅游景区	Guójiā Wǔ'ēi Jí Lǚyóu Jǐngqū	Five A National Tourist Attraction
4. 故宫	Gùgōng	the Imperial Palace, the Forbidden City
5. 长城	Chángchéng	the Great Wall

（一）根据视频内容，选择正确答案 Choose the correct answers according to the video.

（　　）1. 赵丽川去过九寨沟几次了？
　　A. 一次　　　　B. 两次　　　　C. 很多次　　　　D. 没去过

(　　) 2."海子"是当地人对什么的叫法？

　　A. 江　　　B. 河　　　C. 湖　　　D. 海

(　　) 3. 黄龙的风景很美，被叫作什么？

　　A. 世界遗产　　　　B. 天下最美

　　C. 童话世界　　　　D. 人间瑶池

(　　) 4. 以下哪个不是九寨沟和黄龙的共同特点？

　　A. 海拔比较高　　　B. 水的颜色很好看

　　C. 在阿坝州　　　　D. 是国家5A级旅游景区

（二）根据视频内容填空 Fill in the blanks according to the video.

1. 九寨沟有_____的瀑布，还有_____的海子，就像一个童话世界。

2. 从远处看，黄龙就像一条黄色的_____。

3. 黄龙的海拔比较高，有些人在那儿会出现_____。

4. "瑶池"是中国的_____故事里神仙住的地方，当然很美！

5. 到了四川不去九寨沟、黄龙，就像到了北京不去_____、_____一样遗憾！

（三）讨论 Discussion

结束了九寨沟、黄龙的旅行，杜无羡与赵丽川讨论"到底九寨沟和黄龙哪里的水更美"。请你和一位同学分别扮演杜无羡和赵丽川，并在讨论中运用以下词语和结构。

After the trip to Jiuzhai Valley and Huanglong, Du Wuxian and Zhao Lichuan discuss "where is the water more beautiful, Jiuzhai Valley or Huanglong?" Please work in pairs to play the roles of Du Wuxian and Zhao Lichuan respectively, and use the following words and structures in the discussion.

| 风景优美　有特色　迷人　神奇　壮观　五颜六色　五彩斑斓 |
| 流连忘返　　像……一样　　……极了　　太……了 |

相遇天府 Encountering Sichuan: Chinese Video-watching,
——中文视听说 Listening and Speaking

九寨沟风光（Scenery at Jiuzhai Valley）

黄龙风光（Scenery at Huanglong）

任务四（Task Four）

听录音，完成练习 Listen to the recording and do the exercises.

杜无羡、王成和赵丽川讨论暑假旅游的方式。

Du Wuxian, Wang Cheng and Zhao Lichuan are discussing in what way they will travel in the coming summer holiday.

生词和短语（New Words and Expressions）

1. 客运站	kèyùnzhàn	名	passenger station
2. 班车	bānchē	名	regular bus
3. 票价	piàojià	名	price of a ticket
4. 旅游团	lǚyóutuán	名	tour group

续表
Continued

5. 导游	dǎoyóu	名	tour guide
6. 驾照	jiàzhào	名	driver's license
7. 自驾游	zìjiàyóu	动	self-driving tour, road trip
8. 环形	huánxíng	形	ring-shaped, circular
9. 欣赏	xīnshǎng	动	to enjoy, to appriciate
10. 预订	yùdìng	动	to book, to reserve
11. 提前	tíqián	动	to do something in advance or ahead of time
12. 保险	bǎoxiǎn	名	insurance
13. 相机	xiàngjī	名	camera
14. 不停	bùtíng	副	ceaselessly, constantly

专有名词（Proper Names）

1. 松潘	Sōngpān	Songpan County, a county under the jurisdiction of Aba Tibetan and Qiang Autonomous Prefecture in Sichuan Province
2. 江油	Jiāngyóu	Jiangyou City, a city in Sichuan Province

（一）根据录音内容，判断正误 Decide whether the following statements are true or false according to the recording.

(　　) 1. 如果坐飞机去九寨沟，机票比较贵。

(　　) 2. 游客可以在客运站坐大巴去九寨沟。

(　　) 3. 赵丽川没有去过九寨沟。

(　　) 4. 王成没有驾照，不能开车。

(　　) 5. "九环线"是一条很受欢迎的环形旅游路线。

（二）根据录音内容，回答问题 Answer the following questions according to the recording.

1. 王成为什么不想坐飞机去九寨沟？

2. 他们可以坐高铁去九寨沟吗？为什么？

3. 赵丽川觉得参加旅游团怎么样？

4. 他们决定用什么方式去九寨沟旅游？

5. 出发前，他们需要做哪些准备？

（三）小组讨论 Group Discussion

如果你们组的同学们要去九寨沟、黄龙旅游，你们会选择哪种旅游方式？请先分析各种方式的优点和不足，再做出选择。请把讨论的要点写在下面的表中。

If the students in your group were to travel to Jiuzhai Valley and Huanglong, what way of travel would you like to choose? Please analyze the advantages and disadvantages of each way before making a choice. Please write down the key points of the discussion in the table below.

旅游方式	优点	不足
跟团游	1. 导游安排好，很方便。 2. ……	1. 2. ……

（四）口头报告 Oral Presentation

小组代表向全班报告上述讨论的结果，并说一说做出该选择的理由。

The representative of each group reports to the class the results of group discussion and states the reasons for the choice.

语法点注释（Grammar Notes）

1. 如果你有三四天的时间，就可以去川南地区。

"就+动词"表示承接上文，得出结论。

The structure "就+v." indicates a conclusion or a resolution made on the basis of what has been mentioned previously.

① 没有高铁，我们就坐大巴去九寨沟吧。

②"五一"假期不长，我们就在成都附近玩儿吧！

2. 黄龙被叫作"人间瑶池"。

由介词"被"及其宾语做状语的动词谓语句叫"被"字句，说明某人、某事物受到某动作的影响而产生某种结果。其基本格式如下所示。

The sentence with a verb predicate which is modified by the passive preposition"被"and its object as an adverbial adjunct is called the 被-sentence. The

被-sentence expresses that a person or thing is subject to a certain result under the influence of the action. The basic pattern of the 被-sentence is shown below.

受事者 Receiver of the action	介词"被" Preposition "被"	施事者 Doer of the action	动词 Verb	后附成分 （对人、事物的影响和结果） Other elements (the result caused by the action)
主语 Subject	状语 Adverbial adjunct			谓语 Predicate
苹果	被	妹妹	吃	了
我的手机	被	他	摔	坏了
那本书	被	我同学	借	去了

"被"字句中动作的发出者，即施事者，有时可以省略。

The doer of the action sometimes can be omitted.

①他的病被治好了。（一般是指"医生"治好了"他的病"。）

②黄龙被叫作"人间瑶池"。（一般是指"人们"把黄龙叫作"人间瑶池"。）

拓展活动（Extended Activities）

乐行万里

人们常说"读万卷书，行万里路"。"读书"让人增长学识，"行路"让人开拓视野、增长见闻。同学们不但要努力学习知识，有机会还要走出校园去体验和见识世界。

计划一次假期旅行，并与同学们分享你的计划。你的计划中应包括以下要点：

Travelling with Joy

People often say "reading ten thousand books and traveling thousands of miles". "Reading" increases people's knowledge, and "travelling" allows people to broaden their horizons and gain deeper insights. Students not only need to study hard, but also take the opportunity to go out of campus to experience and see the world. Please plan a vacation trip and share your plan with your classmates. Your plan should include the following:

1. 计划什么时候去旅行？
2. 打算跟谁去旅行？
3. 想去什么地方旅行？
4. 这个地方有什么特点？
5. 想选择哪一种旅行方式？为什么？
6. 旅行之前，要做哪些准备？

文化小贴士（Cultural Tips）

中国的法定节假日包括四个传统节日——春节（放假三天）、清明节、端午节和中秋节，以及三个公共假期——元旦节、劳动节和国庆节（放假三天）。如果这些节假日正好在周末前后，那么，一年之中，人们就可能会有几个三天、五天甚至七天的假期。很多人都会在这些假期跟家人、朋友一起去旅行。他们可以选择行程完全由旅行社安排的"跟团游"，也可以选择自己安排吃、住、行，自由选择旅游景点的"自由行"。想要同时享受自由与便利，人们还可以选择由自己安排行程，由旅行社预订机票和酒店的"半自由行"。随着私家车在中国的普及和道路条件的不断改善，越来越多的人开始选择方便又灵活的"自驾游"。当假期来临，人们集中出游，集中消费，也促进了"假日经济"的蓬勃发展。

The legal holidays in China include four traditional festivals: the Spring Festival (a three-day holiday), the Qingming Festival, the Dragon Boat Festival, the Mid-Autumn Festival, and another three public holidays: New Year's Day, May Day, National Day (a three-day holiday). If these holidays happen to be at the preceding or following dates of any weekends, people may have a chance to enjoy a few three-day, five-day, or even seven-day vacations in a year. Many people will travel with their family or friends during these vacations. They can choose a "package tour" where the itinerary is completely arranged by a travel agency, or a "free tour" where people arrange meals, accommodation, transportation all by themselves and choose tourist attractions as they wish. To enjoy both freedom and convenience, people may choose a "semi-free tour" where travelers arrange their own itinerary, and have a travel agency book air tickets and hotels for them. As private cars are getting increasingly common in China and road conditions are constantly getting improved, more and more people are choosing convenient and flexible "self-driving tours". When holidays come, people travel and consume intensively, which, as a result, fosters the boom of a holiday economy.

第六单元 蜀风艺海
Unit 6　Folklore and Featured Art in Sichuan

导入（Lead-in）

你见过哪些四川的民俗活动？你知道四川有什么特别的艺术形式吗？

What folk activities have you ever seen in Sichuan Province? Do you know about any featured art in this province?

任务一（Task One）

看视频，完成练习 Watch the video and do the exercises.

生词和短语（New Words and Expressions）

1.拜年	bài nián	动	to give Chinese New Year greetings, to pay a Chinese New Year visit
2.驰名中外	chímíng-zhōngwài	成	famous and popular at home and abroad
3.春耕	chūngēng	名	spring ploughing
4.大年	dànián	名	the Spring Festival
5.国泰民安	guótài-mín'ān	成	contented people living in a country at peace
6.磕头	kē tóu	动	to kowtow
7.祈求	qíqiú	动	to pray for
8.亲戚	qīn·qi	名	relative
9.清洁	qīngjié	名	cleaning

相遇天府 —— 中文视听说
Encountering Sichuan: Chinese Video-watching, Listening and Speaking

续表
Continued

10.始祖	shǐzǔ	名	earliest ancestor
11.水利	shuǐlì	名	water conservancy, irrigation works
12.五谷丰登	wǔgǔ-fēngdēng	成	an abundant harvest of all crops
13.绣	xiù	名	embroidery
14.扬尘	yángchén	名	flying or hanging dust
15.造福	zàofú	动	to bring benefit to
16.长辈	zhǎngbèi	名	the senior people, elder member of a family

专有名词（Proper Names）

1.都江堰	Dūjiāngyàn	Dujiangyan City, a county-level city of Chengdu City
2.夹江	Jiājiāng	Jiajiang County, a county in Sichuan Province
3.梁平	Liángpíng	Liangping District, a district in Chongqing Municipality
4.绵阳	Miányáng	Mianyang City, a city in Sichuan Province
5.绵竹	Miánzhú	Mianzhu City, a county-level city in Sichuan Province
6.自贡	Zìgòng	Zigong City, a city in Sichuan Province

（一）根据视频内容，回答问题 Answer the following questions according to the video.

1. 什么是"打扬尘"？

2. 什么是"走人户"？

3. 都江堰市为什么每年举办"清明放水节"？

Unit 6　Folklore and Featured Art in Sichuan

4. 广元市的"女儿节"是哪一天？

5. "绵竹年画"有什么特色？

（二）选择与活动对应的节日 Match the activities with corresponding festivals.

　　　　A. 春节　　　B. 清明节　　C. 女儿节　　D. 端午节
（　）1. 女子穿上新衣服，到河边游玩。
（　）2. 小孩子给长辈磕头拜年。
（　）3. 都江堰市放水纪念李冰父子。
（　）4. 去亲戚家"走人户"。

任务二（Task Two）

听录音，完成练习 Listen to the recording and do the exercises.

王成向杜无羡和赵丽川介绍川剧，并邀请他们去观看表演。
Wang Cheng introduces Sichuan Opera to Du Wuxian and Zhao Lichuan, and invites them to watch the performance.

身穿戏服的留学生（International Students in Opera Costumes）

065

相遇天府
——中文视听说
Encountering Sichuan: Chinese Video-watching, Listening and Speaking

生词和短语（New Words and Expressions）

1. 伴奏	bànzòu	动	to accompany with musical instruments
2. 唱腔	chàngqiāng	名	singing tunes in Chinese operas
3. 方言	fāngyán	名	dialect, vernacular
4. 高腔	gāoqiāng	名	a kind of rhyme scheme of Chinese operas
5. 观众	guānzhòng	名	audience
6. 京剧	jīngjù	名	Beijing Opera, Peking Opera
7. 角色	juésè	名	role, part
8. 脸谱	liǎnpǔ	名	facial makeup in traditional Chinese operas
9. 流行	liúxíng	动	to prevail, to be popular
11. 面具	miànjù	名	facial mask
12. 戏曲	xìqǔ	名	traditional Chinese opera
13. 演员	yǎnyuán	名	actor, actress
14. 乐器	yuèqì	名	musical instrument
15. 茶馆	cháguǎn	名	teahouse

专有名词（Proper Names）

重庆	Chóngqìng	Chongqing City, a municipality in southwest China
四川省川剧院	Sìchuānshěng Chuānjùyuàn	Sichuan Opera Troupe

（一）根据录音内容，选择正确答案 Choose the correct answers according to the recording.

（　）1. 杜无美看过川剧吗？
　　A. 看过　　B. 没看过　　C. 他没说　　D. 不想看

（　）2. 川剧和京剧有哪些不同？
　　A. 乐器　　B. 唱腔　　C. 流行的地区　　D. 三个都有

(　　) 3. 变脸是演员改变什么？
　　　A. 面具　　B. 肤色　　　C. 服装　　　D. 灯光

(　　) 4. 最好去哪里看正式的川剧表演？
　　　A. 锦里　　B. 宽窄巷子　　C. 茶馆　　　D. 四川省川剧院

（二）讨论 Discussion

说说你了解的川剧。你还知道中国的哪些剧种呢？

Share your knowledge of Sichuan Opera and any other Chinese operas you have known about.

任务三（Task Three）

看视频，完成练习 Watch the video and do the exercises.

成都博物馆（Chengdu Museum）

相遇天府——中文视听说

Encountering Sichuan: Chinese Video-watching, Listening and Speaking

生词和短语（New Words and Expressions）

1. 场面	chǎngmiàn	名	occasion, scene
2. 顿	dùn	量	for times of meals or beating
3. 红白喜事	hóng bái xǐshì	名	weddings and funerals
4. 讲究	jiǎng·jiu	动、形、名	to be particular about, to stress; posh; rules of etiquette
5. 亲朋好友	qīnpéng hǎoyǒu	短	relatives and friends
6. 食材	shícái	名	ingredient, food material
7. 宴席	yànxí	名	banquet, feast
8. 由于	yóuyú	介	owing to, because of
9. 蒸	zhēng	形	steamed (dishes)
10. 左邻右舍	zuǒlín-yòushè	成	next-door neighbors

专有名词（Proper Names）

1. 坝坝宴	Bà·bayàn	banquet in the courtyard
2. 咸烧白	Xián Shāobái	Sichuan-style steamed pork with pickled mustard leaves

（一）根据视频内容，回答问题 Answer the following questions according to the video.

1. 成都人什么时候摆"坝坝宴"？

2. 成都人会用"坝坝宴"宴请谁？

3. "斗碗"在四川方言里是什么意思？

第六单元 蜀风艺海
Unit 6 Folklore and Featured Art in Sichuan

4. 穷人家的"坝坝宴"摆几碗？

（二）讨论 Discussion

谈谈你知道的川菜的口味和特色吧，例如：宫保鸡丁、麻婆豆腐、麻辣火锅……

Share your knowledge about flavors and features of Sichuan dishes. for example: Kung Pao Chicken, Mother Chen's Tofu, Sichuan Hotpot, etc.

任务四（Task Four）

听录音，完成练习 Listen to the recording and do the exercises.

赵丽川带杜无羡去一家小店买拖鞋，还教了他几句四川方言。

Zhao Lichuan takes Du Wuxian to buy slippers in a store, and teaches him a few words in Sichuan dialect.

生词和短语（New Words and Expressions）

1. 巴适	bāshi	形	a word in Sichuan dialect with the meaning of "comfortable" or "feeling good"
2. 相因	xiāngyīn	形	a word in Sichuan dialect with the meaning of "cheap"

（一）听录音，选择与四川话发音对应的意思 Listen to the recording, and match the sounds in Sichuan dialect with corresponding expressions.

( ) 1. haizi　　　　A. 小孩　　B. 好朋友　　C. 鞋子　　D. 大海

( ) 2. xiangyin　　A. 便宜　　B. 相信　　C. 原因　　D. 好吃

( ) 3. bashi de hen A. 爸爸　　B. 汽车　　C. 很凶　　D. 很好

069

（二）角色扮演 Role-play

和同学分角色表演这个对话，加上一些自己会的四川方言词汇。

Act out the dialogue with classmates. Other acquired expressions in Sichuan dialect may be added to the story.

语法点注释（Grammar Notes）

1. 一方面是为了纪念李冰父子，他们二人在2200多年前带领大家修建都江堰水利工程，造福成都平原；另一方面也象征着一年春耕的开始，人们祈求五谷丰登、国泰民安。

联合关系的并列复句(Coordinative Relation in Coordinate Complex Sentences)
并列复句中的几个分句分别说明、描写几件事情或者说明同一事物的几个方面。

The clauses in coordinate complex sentences explain or describe several things respectively or explain the different aspects of one thing. For example,

①过年一方面象征着家庭团圆，另一方面象征着辞旧迎新。
②四川民俗文化一方面是中国民俗文化的一部分，另一方面又有自己的特色。

2. 在中国文化里，数字"九"表示数量多，而"斗碗"在四川方言里就是"大碗"的意思。所以"九斗碗"的意思就是摆了很多道菜的宴席。

因果关系的偏正复句(Causative Relation in Subordinate Complex Sentences)
偏正复句中的偏句说出原因或前提，正句说出结果或根据前提做出的推断。

The subordinate clauses in the subordinate complex sentences state the reason or premises while the main clauses state the result or inference drawn from the premises.

① 由于宴席是摆在自家的院子里，所以叫作"坝坝宴"。
② 因为川剧中的"变脸"很有意思，所以很多人都喜欢观看。

扩展活动（Extended Activities）

去成都博物馆、四川博物院、金沙遗址博物馆和川菜博物馆了解更多的四川民俗和特色艺术，选择你最感兴趣的民俗或特色艺术并录制一段5分钟的视频（形式不限），在班里跟大家分享。

Visit Chengdu Museum, Sichuan Museum, Jinsha Relics Museum, and Museum of Sichuan Cuisine, find out more about folklore and featured art in Sichuan. Record a 5-minute video (with styles unlimited) based on features of folklore or art that interest you the most, and share with the class.

分享提纲（Possible topics for sharing）
1. 成都博物馆最重要的展品是什么？
2. 四川博物馆与成都博物馆有哪些不同？
3. 金沙遗址博物馆里除了文物还有什么特色？
4. 川菜博物馆能学做川菜吗？

文化小贴士（Cultural Tips）

非物质文化遗产是指各族人民世代相传并视为其文化遗产组成部分的各种传统文化表现形式，以及与传统文化表现形式相关的实物和场所。非物质文化遗产包括：（一）传统口头文学以及作为其载体的语言；（二）传统美术、书法、音乐、舞蹈、戏剧、曲艺和杂技；（三）传统技艺、医药和历法；（四）传统礼仪、节庆等民俗；（五）传统体育和游艺；（六）其他非物质文化遗产。四川素有"天府之国"的美誉，世居于此的各族人民用勤劳和智慧创造了绚丽多彩的非物质文化遗产，包括苗族古歌、羌族羊皮鼓舞、四川皮影戏、四川竹琴、峨眉武术、蜀锦织造技艺、蒙山茶传统制作技艺、成都中药炮制技术等。这些宝贵的财富是中华优秀传统文化的重要组成部分，是巴蜀文化绵延传承的生动见证，具有重要的历史意义和时代价值。

Intangible cultural heritage refers to various traditional cultural expressions that have been passed down from generation to generation by people of all ethnic groups and are considered as part of their cultural heritage, as well as the physical objects and places associated with traditional cultural expressions. Intangible cultural heritage includes: (a) traditional oral literature and the language used as its carrier; (b) traditional art, calligraphy, music, dance, drama, opera and acrobatics; (c) traditional arts, medicine and calendars; (d) traditional rituals, festivals and other folk customs; (e) traditional sports and amusement; and (f) other intangible cultural heritage. Sichuan is known as the Land of Heaven, and the people of all ethnic groups living here have created a rich intangible cultural heritage with diligence and wisdom, including: Miao ancient ballads, Qiang sheepskin drumming, Sichuan shadow play, Sichuan bamboo string instrument, Emei martial arts, Shu brocade weaving techniques, Mengshan Mountain traditional tea production techniques, Chengdu Chinese medicine concoction techniques, etc. These valuable treasures are an important part of the excellent Chinese traditional culture, a vivid continuous transmission of the Shu culture, and have important historical significance and value of the times.

第七单元　百味物语
Unit 7　Sichuan Cuisine

导入（Lead-in）

你吃过哪些川菜？你最喜欢哪一种？为什么？
What Sichuan food have you ever eaten? Which is your favorite and why?

任务一（Task One）

看视频，完成练习 Watch the video and do the exercises.

生词和短语（New Words and Expressions）

1. 作为	zuòwéi	介	as
2. 代表	dàibiǎo	名	representative
3. 菜系	càixì	名	style of cooking
4. 味道	wèidào	名	taste
5. 独特	dútè	形	unique
6. 闻名	wénmíng	形	famous
7. 特点	tèdiǎn	名	characteristics
8. 广泛	guǎngfàn	形	extensive
9. 山珍	shānzhēn	名	delicacy from mountains
10. 河鲜	héxiān	名	delicacy from rivers

073

续表
Continued

11. 基本	jīběn		形	basic
12. 麻	má		形	tongue-numbing
13. 辣	là		形	spicy
14. 咸	xián		形	salty
15. 甜	tián		形	sweet
16. 酸	suān		形	sour
17. 组合	zǔhé		名、动	combination; to combine
18. 烹饪	pēngrèn		动	to cook
19. 至少	zhìshǎo		副	at least
20. 炒	chǎo		动	to stir-fry
21. 烧	shāo		动	to braise
22. 炖	dùn		动	to stew
23. 煮	zhǔ		动	to boil
24. 小吃	xiǎochī		名	snack
25. 伤心	shāngxīn		形	heart-broken
26. 凉粉	liángfěn		名	bean jelly
27. 浑	hún		形	turbid
28. 沾	zhān		动	to stick to
29. 火锅	huǒguō		名	hotpot
30. 串串	chuànchuan		名	clusters: a kind of spicy hot snack
31. 冒菜	màocài		名	instant spicy steampot
32. 制作	zhìzuò		动	to make
33. 其中	qízhōng		名	among (which, them, etc.)
34. 名片	míngpiàn		名	name card, business card
35. 介绍	jièshào		动	to introduce

专有名词（Proper Names）

1. 回锅肉	Huíguō Ròu	Double-fried Pork Slices
2. 麻婆豆腐	Mápó Dòufu	Stir-Fried Tofu in Hot Sauce
3. 宫保鸡丁	Gōngbǎo Jīdīng	Diced Chicken with Paprika
4. 糖醋排骨	Tángcù Páigǔ	Sweet and Sour Spare Ribs
5. 怪味鸡	Guàiwèi Jī	Special Flavored Shredded Chicken
6. 赖汤圆	Lài tāngyuán	Lai Glutinous Rice Balls

（一）根据视频内容，判断正误 Decide whether the following statements are true or false according to the video.

(　　) 1. 回锅肉是川菜的一个代表。
(　　) 2. 川菜的基本味道有四种。
(　　) 3. 宫保鸡丁又麻又辣。
(　　) 4. 川菜的烹饪方法有一百多种。
(　　) 5. 火锅是四川的名片。

（二）根据视频内容填空 Fill in the blanks according to the video.

1. 作为中国_____大菜系之一的川菜，味道独特，全国_____，所以有"食在中国，味在四川"的说法。

2. 川菜的特点是：食材广泛，做法多样，_____菜_____味。

3. 怪味鸡混合了麻、辣、咸、_____、酸。

4. 四川还有_____小吃，比如，辣得让人"流泪"的_____凉粉、"煮时不浑汤，吃时_____不沾"的赖汤圆和制作时_____发出"砰、砰、砰"三声响的"三大炮"。

5. 到了四川如果不吃_____，就等于没有到过四川。

任务二（Task Two）

听录音，完成练习 Listen to the recording and do the exercises.

杜无羡去王成家，看到赵丽川和王成正在做火锅。
Du Wuxian goes to Wang Cheng's home and sees he is making hotpot with Zhao Lichuan.

白锅锅底（Plain Broth）

红锅锅底（Spicy Broth）

鸳鸯锅锅底（Double-flavor Hot Pot）

肥牛（Beef Slides）

生词和短语（New Words and Expressions）

1. 需要	xūyào	动	to need
2. 准备	zhǔnbèi	动	to prepare
3. 调料	tiáoliào	名	seasoning, condiment
4. 锅底	guōdǐ	名	hotpot seasoning

续表
Continued

5. 潮湿	cháoshī	形	humid
6. 容易	róngyì	形	likely
7. 出汗	chūhàn	动	to sweat
8. 湿气	shīqì	名	moisture
9. 寒气	hánqì	名	coldness
10. 原来	yuánlái	副	actually, originally
11. 看来	kànlái	动	to appear
12. 烫	tàng	动	to boil food briefly
13. 肥牛	féiniú	名	beef slides
14. 毛肚	máodǔ	名	tripe
15. 鸭肠	yācháng	名	duck intestine

（一）根据录音内容，判断正误 Decide whether the following statements are true or false according to the recording.

(　　) 1. 四川人都很喜欢吃辣的东西。

(　　) 2. 冬天多吃辣椒不容易生病。

(　　) 3. 杜无美不知道怎么吃火锅。

(　　) 4. 吃火锅时一般先吃菜再吃肉。

（二）根据录音内容，选择正确答案 Choose the correct answers according to the recording.

(　　) 1. 四川人喜欢吃辣椒主要和什么有关系？
　　　　A. 习惯　　　B. 气候　　　C. 爱好　　　D. 地理

(　　) 2. 吃火锅一般需要什么？
　　　　A. 肉　　　　B. 蔬菜　　　C. 锅底　　　D. A、B 和 C

（　　）3. 四川的冬天天气怎么样？
　　　　A. 干燥　　　　B. 阴冷　　　　C. 温暖　　　　D. 湿热
（　　）4. 冬天吃饭时如果全身出汗，什么会跟着汗水一起排出来？
　　　　A. 湿气　　　　B. 冷气　　　　C. 寒气　　　　D. A和C
（　　）5. 烫肥牛时，数到几就可以吃了？
　　　　A. 十五　　　　B. 二十　　　　C. 二十五　　　D. 三十

（三）问答 Answering questions

吃火锅时，下面的哪些食物需要煮，哪些食物需要烫？
肥牛　　牛肉　　土豆　　鸭肠　　毛肚

（四）讨论 Discussion

吃火锅时，在下列菜单中你会选择什么锅底和食物？为什么？

菜单	
荤菜	素菜
1. 肥牛　38元（　　） 2. 毛肚　28元（　　） 3. 鸭肠　28元（　　） 4. 排骨　30元（　　） 5. 鸡肉　28元（　　） 6. 牛肉　38元（　　） 7. 羊肉　38元（　　） 8. 虾　　48元（　　）	1. 土豆　8元（　　） 2. 黄瓜　6元（　　） 3. 豆腐　10元（　　） 4. 豆芽　6元（　　） 5. 青菜　8元（　　） 6. 香菇　12元（　　） 7. 南瓜　8元（　　） 8. 藕　　8元（　　）
锅底	
1. 菌汤鸳鸯锅　38元（　　） 2. 番茄鸳鸯锅　38元（　　） 3. 红锅锅底　　28元（　　） 4. 白锅锅底　　28元（　　）	

Unit 7　Sichuan Cuisine

任务三（Task Three）

看视频，完成练习 Watch the video and do the exercises.

赵丽川、丹枫和华锦在饭馆外面讨论四川菜。
Zhao Lichuan, Dan Feng and Hua Jin are talking about Sichuan food outside a restaurant.

辣子鸡（Peppery Chicken）　　　　鱼香肉丝（Fish-flavored Pork）

生词和短语（New Words and Expressions）

1. 实际上	shíjì·shàng	副	in fact	
2. 鱼香	yúxiāng	名	a taste made from pickled chili, onions, ginger, sugar, salt, etc.	
3. 五香	wǔxiāng	名	the five kinds of seasoning: fennel, zanthoxylum, aniseed, cinnamon, clove	
4. 问题	wèntí	名	problem	
5. 受	shòu	动	to receive, to accept	
6. 欢迎	huānyíng	动	to welcome	
7. 挺	tǐng	副	rather	
8. 稍微	shāowēi	副	a little	
9. 好像	hǎoxiàng	副	seemingly	
10. 刺	cì	名	bone (of the fish)	
11. 麻烦	máfan	形	troublesome	

续表
Continued

12. 腥味	xīngwèi	名	fishy smell
13. 担心	dān xīn	动	to worry about
14. 奇怪	qíguài	形	weird, strange
15. 清楚	qīng·chu	形	clear

专有名词（Proper Names）

1. 辣子鸡	Làzi Jī	Peppery Chicken
2. 糖醋里脊	Tángcù Lǐjǐ	Sweet and Sour Fillet

（一）根据视频内容，将下列食物和其味道搭配起来 Match the food below to their tastes according to the video.

1. 辣子鸡　　　　a. 麻
2. 麻婆豆腐　　　b. 酸甜
3. 宫保鸡丁　　　c. 甜辣
4. 糖醋里脊　　　d. 不清楚
5. 鱼香肉丝　　　e. 辣

（二）根据视频内容，判断正误 Decide whether the following statements are true or false according to the video.

(　) 1. 丹枫今天不想再吃川菜了。
(　) 2. 华锦昨天吃了辣子鸡。
(　) 3. 除了辣味和麻味，川菜没有其他味道了。
(　) 4. 鱼香肉丝里没有鱼。
(　) 5. 他们最后点了三道菜。

（三）根据视频内容，回答问题 Answer the following questions according to the video.

1. 哪道菜很多留学生都喜欢吃？

2. 赵丽川觉得鱼香肉丝的味道像什么呢？

_____

（四）自创川菜 Sihcuan Dish Creation

三个同学一组，利用所学的知识，自创一道川菜。写下这道菜的原料、佐料和烹饪方法，并描述这道菜的风味。

Form a group of three students and create a Sichuan dish with what you have learnt. Write down your recipe of the dish, including the ingredients, seasoning and the cooking methods, and describe the flavor of the dish.

任务四（Task Four）

听录音，完成练习 Listen to the recording and do the exercises.

赵丽川给丹枫和杜无羡介绍四川的小吃。
Zhao Lichuan is introducing Sichuan snacks to Dan Feng and Du Wuxian.

蛋烘糕（Baked Egg Cake）　　钵钵鸡（Bobo Chicken）

相遇天府
——中文视听说
Encountering Sichuan: Chinese Video-watching, Listening and Speaking

夫妻肺片（Sliced Beef and Ox Tongue in Chili Sauce）

担担面（Dan Dan Noodles）

钟水饺（Zhong Dumpling）

生词和短语（New Words and Expressions）

1.移民	yímín	名、动	immigrant; to migrate
2.有关	yǒuguān	动	to concern, to have something to do with
3.故乡	gùxiāng	名	hometown
4.思念	sīniàn	动	to miss
5.家乡	jiāxiāng	名	hometown
6.特别	tèbié	副	especially
7.以为	yǐwéi	动	to think, to believe
8.遇到	yùdào	动	to encounter
9.口感	kǒugǎn	名	flavor

续表
Continued

10.发明	fāmíng	动	to invent
11.牛杂	niúzá	名	essence of beef offal
12.扁担	biǎndan	名	carrying or shoulder pole
13.挑	tiāo	动	to carry
14.馅儿	xiànr	名	stuffing
15.纯	chún	形	pure

专有名词（Proper Names）

1. 蛋烘糕	Dànhōnggāo	Baked Egg Cake
2. 钵钵鸡	Bōbō Jī	Bobo Chicken
3. 夫妻肺片	Fūqī Fèipiàn	Sliced Beef and Ox Tongue in Chili Sauce
4. 担担面	Dàndan Miàn	Dan Dan Noodles
5. 钟水饺	Zhōng Shuǐjiǎo	Zhong Dumpling

（一）根据录音内容，判断正误 Decide whether the following statements are true or false according to the recording.

（　　） 1. 夫妻肺片是一对夫妻发明的。
（　　） 2. 夫妻肺片里面主要是牛肉和牛肺。
（　　） 3. 牛肺的口感还不错。

（二）根据录音内容填空 Fill in the blanks according to the recording.

1. 伤心凉粉是四川的一种小吃，和移民到四川的客家人＿＿＿＿＿＿。客家人的故乡在广东，他们思念＿＿＿＿＿＿时会做凉粉，因为思念而伤心，所以叫伤心凉粉。还有一种说法是：伤心凉粉＿＿＿＿＿＿辣，吃的时候会辣出眼泪，别人还＿＿＿＿＿＿遇到了什么伤心事。

2. 担担面，＿＿＿＿＿＿是用扁担挑在肩上去卖，所以叫担担面。

3. 中国北方的水饺馅儿里面一般都有_____，但是钟水饺是纯_____馅儿的。

（三）讨论 Discussion

根据文中的图片，谈谈自己最喜欢的四川小吃。

Talk about your favorite Sichuan snacks according to the pictures given in the text.

语法点注释（Grammar Notes）

1. 川菜的基本味道有五种，川菜的烹饪方法至少有几十种。
动词"有"表示达到（某个数量）。
The verb "有" expresses the meaning of reaching a certain amount.
① 这道菜的调料有四五种。
② 在成都，他开的火锅店有十几家。

2. 昨天朋友请我吃了辣子鸡，辣得我眼泪都流出来了！
副词"都"表示程度"甚至"。
The adverb "都" expresses the degree, meaning 'even'.
① 吃完辣子鸡，嘴唇都变大了！
② 天气热得我都不想吃火锅了。

3. 宫保鸡丁听起来挺好的。
听起来/看起来表示听到或者看到某种情况后的感觉和印象，常用于推断。
Sensory verb+起来 is used to express the feeling and impression of somebody who has heard or seen something, usually indicting inferences.
① 糖醋里脊听起来不错。
② 冒菜看起来很辣。

4. 别人还以为遇到了什么伤心事。
疑问代词"什么"表示虚指，可以在句子中去掉。
The interrogative pronoun "什么" indicates nothing, and can be deleted in a sentence.

① 你这么做回锅肉，没有什么味道。
② 吃太多辣椒，不是什么好事。

5. 是不是就是中国北方的水饺？

"是不是"在汉语中表示疑问词。它同时包含两种含义："是"与"不是"。一种是对问题的确定，一种是对问题的否认，综合在一起就是对事情的确定和否认所提出的疑问。

"是不是" is used to indicate an interrogative sentence in Chinese. This structure covers two meanings：'yes' and 'no'. It both affirms and negates a statement, so it poses as a question to a statement.

① 抄手是不是水饺？——不是。
② 你是不是饿了？——是，我饿了。

扩展活动（Extended Activities）

美食分享

趁周末和假期亲自去调查并品尝一下四川还有什么美食，用简单的中文介绍一下它的原材料以及色、香、味，并录制成视频，分享给大家。

Gourmet Food Sharing

Conduct a survey and try in person some other Sichuan food at weekends or during holidays. Video this food and introduce its raw materials, taste, smell, color, etc. in simple Chinese. Video it and share it with your classmates.

文化小贴士（Cultural Tips）

川菜有什么魅力呢？一是其菜品本身的味道。川菜麻辣鲜香、口味重，能下饭，一下饭之后人一吃饱就会觉得浑身舒畅。二是其人味儿。川菜的味道造就了四川人独特的性格：泼辣、顽强。泼辣是因为四川人很能吃辣椒，辣椒能促进血液循环，使人精力充沛、情绪亢奋、敢拼敢闯。顽强是因为无论生活多么困难、条件如何艰苦，四川人总能在天上、水里、地上找到吃的，而且还能做得色香味俱全。

  The charm of Sichuan Cuisine lies first in its taste. The unique strong taste of Sichuan Cuisine characterized by hot and numbing makes it uniquely go well with rice. One will feel satisfied and comfortable once he or she is full. The Charm of Sichuan Cuisine lies secondly in its humanity. Sichuan people are of a hot-temper and strong will. Sichuan people love pepper. Pepper, one eaten, will improve blood circulation which makes people energetic, excited and adventurous. In addition, no matter how hard life is and conditions are, Sichuan people can always figure out ways to find food available from the sky, the river and the land, making it delicious, which results in their indomitable spirit.

第八单元 蓉城茶香
Unit 8　Sichuan Tea Culture

导入（Lead-in）

你在四川喝过茶吗？四川有哪些有名的茶叶和茶馆？

Have you ever had tea in Sichuan? What are the famous teas and tea houses in Sichuan?

蒙顶山茶树
（Tea Trees in Mengding Mountain）

任务一（Task One）

看视频，完成练习 Watch the video and do the exercises.

生词和短语（New Words and Expressions）

1. 产地	chǎndì	名	place of production
2. 野生	yěshēng	形	wild

续表
Continued

3. 种植	zhòngzhí	动	to plant
4. 甚至	shènzhì	副	even, indeed
5. 俗话说	súhuà shuō	短	as the saying goes
6. 数	shǔ	动	to count
7. 打盹儿	dǎ dǔnr	动	to take a nap
8. 闲书	xiánshū	名	light reading
9. 掏耳朵	tāo ěrduo	动	to pick the ears
10. 算命	suàn mìng	动	to tell fortune
11. 看相	kàn xiàng	动	to physiognomize
12. 自在	zì·zai	形	free, at ease
13. 茶具	chájù	名	tea set
14. 体现	tǐxiàn	动	to embody
15. 迷人	mírén	形	charming, enchanting
16. 魅力	mèilì	名	charm
17. 悠闲	yōuxián	形	leisurely, laidback, easygoing

专有名词（Proper Names）

1. 峨眉毛峰	Éméi Máofēng	a green tea produced in Emei Mountain
2. 蒙顶甘露	Méngdǐng Gānlù	a green tea produced in Mengding Mountain
3. 青城雪芽	Qīngchéng Xuěyá	a green tea produced in Qingcheng Mountain
4. 峨眉竹叶青	Éméi Zhúyèqīng	a green tea produced in Emei Mountain

（一）根据视频内容，判断正误 Decide whether the following statements are true or false according to the video.

（　　）1. 四川是最早发现有茶的地方之一。

（　　）2. 四川的茶特别好喝，是因为四川在中国的南方。

第八单元 蓉城茶香
Unit 8 Sichuan Tea Culture

（　　）3. 峨眉竹叶青不是四川有名的茶。
（　　）4. 四川的茶馆比中国其他地方的茶馆都多。
（　　）5. 在四川的一些茶馆里可以看川剧。

（二）根据视频内容填空 Fill in the blanks according to the video.

1. 中国是茶树的_____，茶叶的_____，是世界上_____最早的国家。

2. 四川被认为是中国甚至世界_____、_____、_____茶叶的起源地之一。

3. 四川有很多_____，有良好的_____和_____，所以四川的茶也特别好喝。

4. 有时候，旁边还有_____的、_____的、_____的，大家都很开心自在。

5. 川茶体现了四川文化_____，体现了四川人_____。

任务二（Task Two）

听录音，完成练习 Listen to the recording and do the exercises.

杜无羡、丹枫和中国朋友赵丽川聊成都的特色茶馆。
Du Wuxian, Dan Feng and their Chinese friend Zhao Lichuan are talking about the teahouses with Chengdu characteristics.

坝坝茶（Baba Tea）

生词和短语（New Words and Expressions）

1. 适合	shìhé	动	to fit, to suit
2. 露天	lùtiān	副	outdoors
3. 场地	chǎngdì	名	venue, yard
4. 晒	shài	动	to bask, to sunbathe
5. 矮桌	ǎi zhuō	短	low table
6. 平民	píngmín	名	common people
7. 消费	xiāofèi	动	to consume

（一）根据录音内容，判断正误 Decide whether the following statements are true or false according to the recording.

（　）1. 天晴的时候，四川人喜欢去茶馆喝茶。
（　）2. "坝坝茶"不是一种茶的名字。
（　）3. 坝坝的意思是茶馆里的场地。
（　）4. "摆龙门阵"是一句四川方言，就是聊天的意思。
（　）5. 平民消费就是不贵的意思。

（二）讨论 Discussion

说一说在你们国家喝茶和在四川喝茶有什么不一样。
What's the difference between drinking tea in your country and in Sichuan?

任务三（Task Three）

看视频，完成练习 Watch the video and do the exercises.

乔筝和杜无羡去茶馆喝茶，听茶博士静妹儿介绍四川茶和盖碗茶。
Qiao Zheng and Du Wuxian go to drink tea in a teahouse and listen to the tea master Ms. Jing introduce Sichuan tea and Gaiwan tea.

第八单元 蓉城茶香
Unit 8 Sichuan Tea Culture

汝瓷（Ru Porcelain）

盖碗茶（Gaiwan Tea）

生词和短语（New Words and Expressions）

1.茶单	chádān	名	tea menu
2.著名	zhùmíng	形	famous
3.竹叶	zhúyè	名	bamboo leaf
4.起伏	qǐfú	动、形	to rise and fall; ups and downs
5.茶盖	chágài	名	tea lid
6.茶碗	cháwǎn	名	tea bowl
7.品	pǐn	动	to sample, to taste
8.茶礼	chálǐ	名	tea etiquette
9.动作	dòngzuò	名	action
10.三吹三浪	sānchuī sānlàng	短	to make the lid of the bowl submerged in the water and push it three times and then drink the tea in three times
11.翻	fān	动	to turn over
12.杯沿	bēiyán	名	rim of a cup
13.平放	píngfàng	动	to lay... flat
14.暂时	zànshí	形	temporary

091

专有名词（Proper Names）

汝瓷	Rǔcí	Ru Porcelain

（一）根据视频内容，选择正确答案 Choose the correct answers according to the video.

（　　）1. 乔筝和杜无美选了茶单上的什么茶？
　　A. 蒙顶甘露
　　B. 峨眉竹叶青
　　C. 碧潭飘雪
　　D. 蒙顶黄芽

（　　）2. 下面哪一个不是竹叶青的特点？
　　A. 竹叶青的产地是峨眉
　　B. 竹叶青是红茶
　　C. 竹叶青看起来像竹叶
　　D. 最好用玻璃杯泡竹叶青

（　　）3. 下列哪个不是碧潭飘雪的特点？
　　A. 茶汤很绿
　　B. 茶里面加了一种花
　　C. 花在茶汤上面像一片片白雪
　　D. 碧潭飘雪的名字和产地有关

（　　）4. 哪一个动作是喝盖碗茶时买单的意思？
　　A. 把茶盖翻过来，放在杯沿
　　B. 把茶盖翻过来放在茶碗的上面
　　C. 把茶盖平放在碗旁
　　D. 用手指敲桌子

（二）角色扮演 Role-play

两个同学一组，一个是茶博士，另一个是顾客，表演如何泡和喝盖碗茶。

Pair work: one is a customer and the other is a tea master. You show how to make and drink Gaiwan tea.

任务四（Task Four）

听对话，完成练习 Listen to the dialogue and do the exercises.

何蓉蓉打电话问王成怎样才能买到好茶叶。
He Rongrong calls Wang Cheng to ask how to buy good tea.

特级绿茶（Extra Grade Green Tea）

生词和短语（New Words and Expressions）

1. 礼物	lǐwù	名	gift, present
2. 请教	qǐngjiào	动	to consult, to seek advice
3. 记	jì	动	to write, to note
4. 品质	pǐnzhì	名	quality
5. 差别	chābié	名	difference
6. 淡绿	dànlǜ	形	light green
7. 鲜	xiān	形	fresh
8. 大小	dàxiǎo	名	size
9. 均匀	jūnyún	形	even, uniform
10. 碎	suì	形	fragmentary, full of bits
11. 等级	děngjí	名	grade, class
12. 特级	tèjí	形	extra grade, superfine

相遇天府
——中文视听说
Encountering Sichuan: Chinese Video-watching, Listening and Speaking

（一）两人一组为视频中的活动配音 Two students work together to dub the video.

（二）口语练习 Speaking Practice

怎样才能买到好的茶叶？
How can one buy good tea?

语法点注释（Grammar Notes）

1. 把茶盖翻过来。

由介词"把"及其宾语做状语的动词谓语句叫"把"字句，表示对某人、某事物施加某种动作并强调使某人、某事物产生某种结果或影响。基本格式是：实施者+介词"把"+受事者+动词+后附成分（人、事物受到的影响或结果）。

A sentence with a verb predicate modified by the preposition "把" and its object is called the 把 sentence. The 把 sentence indicates that an action is applied to somebody or something with the emphasis that the action will bring about a result or influence. The basic pattern is: Doer of the action+the proposition "把"+ Receiver of the action +verb+other elements (the result caused by the action).

①我把您要的四川茶叶给您带来了。
②把我的盖碗茶放在里面的桌子上。

2. 上面的茉莉花像片片白雪。

如果表示两个人或两种事物相像，可以用动词"像"引出比较对象，或后面再用谓语表示比较的方面或标准。

To express that two presents or things are similar, the verb "像" may be used to introduce the one as the standard of comparison. The predicate of such a sentence tells the aspect of comparison.

①这种茶叶泡好后像一根根银针。
②这个汝瓷茶杯很漂亮，对着阳光看，里面像星星一样。

扩展活动 (Extended Activities)

邀请你的朋友在天晴的时候一起去成都有名的坝坝茶馆体验四川有名的盖碗茶,并录制视频,在课堂上分享。

Invite your friends to go to Chengdu's famous Baba teahouses on a sunny day to experience Sichuan's famous Gaiwan Tea. Make a video and share your experience in class.

文化小贴士 (Cultural Tips)

1. 盖碗茶 (Gaiwan Tea)

四川茶馆里最常见的便是"盖碗茶",这也是成都最先发明的特色饮茶形式。所谓"盖碗茶",包括茶盖、茶碗、茶船子三部分,故称盖碗。茶船子,又叫茶舟,即承受茶碗的茶托子。"盖碗茶"相传是唐代德宗建中年间(780—783年)由西川节度使崔宁之女在成都发明的。这种特有的饮茶方式逐步由巴蜀向四周地区浸润发展,后来遍及整个南方。

The most common form of tea in Sichuan teahouses is "Gaiwan Tea", which was first invented in Chengdu. The so-called "Lid bowl tea" includes three parts: a tea lid (gai in Chinese), a tea bowl (wan in Chinese) and a tea boat, so it is called Gaiwan. Tea boat is used to bear the tea bowl. It is said that it was invented in Chengdu by Cui Ning, the daughter of Xichuan governor, during the reign of Zong Jianzhong (780-783) of the Tang Dynasty. This unique way of drinking tea gradually spread from Sichuan to the surrounding areas, and later spread throughout the southern China.

2. 摆龙门阵 (Sichuan style chatting)

"龙门阵"是名词,就是聊天的意思,"摆龙门阵"就是进行聊天的意思。摆龙门阵就是几个人相聚、玩耍、做活时讲故事、聊天、闲谈、神吹、侃大山的文化活动。显然,龙门阵不同于一般聊天的地方,就在于它必须极尽铺陈、排比、夸张、联想之能事。

"Long men zhen" is a noun, meaning to chat, and "bai long men zhen" means to conduct the chatting. It is a cultural activity for several people to get together, to play, to do work, to tell stories, to chat, to blow, to shoot the breeze. Obviously, "long men zhen" is different from the general chat because it must make the most of the presentation, comparison, exaggeration, and the association of things.

第九单元 快享慢活
Unit 9　Contemporary Lifestyle in Chengdu

导入（Lead-in）

你在成都见过哪些特别的生活方式？你是否喜欢这些生活习惯？

What special lifestyle or activities have you ever seen in Chengdu? Do you like these life habits or cultural phenomena?

任务一（Task One）

看视频，完成练习 Watch the video and do the exercises.

生词和短语（New Words and Expressions）

1. 快捷	kuàijié	形	easy and fast
2. 外卖	wàimài	名	takeaway food
3. 平和	pínghé	形	peaceful
4. 安逸	ānyì	形	easy and comfortable
5. 节奏	jiézòu	名	tempo
6. 广场舞	guǎngchǎngwǔ	名	square dance
7. 郊区	jiāoqū	名	suburb
8. 农家乐	nóngjiālè	名	agritainment, countryside recreation

续表
Continued

| 9. 新鲜 | xīnxiān | 形 | fresh |
| 10. 气质 | qìzhì | 名 | temperament |

专有名词（Proper Names）

1. 微信	Wēixìn	WeChat
2. 支付宝	Zhīfùbǎo	Alipay
3. 滴滴	Dīdī	Didi App, a shared taxi app
4. 抖音	Dǒuyīn	Chinese TikTok

（一）根据视频内容，判断正误 Decide whether the following statements are true or false according to the video.

（　　）1. 成都人的生活都是快节奏的。
（　　）2. 微信、支付宝等应用程序使生活更加便捷。
（　　）3. 成都人喜欢安逸的生活方式。
（　　）4. 相比成都人，上海人更喜欢去农家乐。

（二）根据图片内容，选择相应的活动 Match the picture with corresponding activities.

1. 打麻将（　　） 2. 去农家乐（　　） 3. 跳广场舞（　　） 4. 喝茶（　　）

A.

B.

C.

D.

任务二 (Task Two)

听录音，完成练习 Listen to the conversation and do the exercises.

王成、林一诺和杜无羡在通过视频电话聊各类线上应用软件。

Wang Cheng, Lin Yinuo and Du Wuxian are talking about different online apps on a video call.

生词和短语 (New Words and Expressions)

1. 在线视频	zàixiàn shìpín	短	online video call
2. 视频	shìpín	名	video
3. 距离	jùlí	名	distance
4. 酒吧	jiǔbā	名	bar
5. 电子产品	diànzǐ chǎnpǐn	短	electronic product
6. 网站	wǎngzhàn	名	website
7. 网络	wǎngluò	名	network
8. 分享	fēnxiǎng	动	to share
9. 多姿多彩	duōzī duōcǎi	短	colorful and various
10. 占用	zhànyòng	动	to occupy
11. 不错	búcuò	形	not bad
12. 商业模式	shāngyè móshì	短	business model
13. 创业	chuàngyè	动	to start businesses

专有名词 (Proper Names)

1. 成都339	Chéngdū Sānsānjiǔ	Chengdu 339, a bar zone in Chengdu
2. 京东	Jīngdōng	Jingdong, an online shopping mall
3. 淘宝	Táobǎo	Taobao, an online shopping mall

第九单元　慢享快活
Unit 9　Contemporary Lifestyle in Chengdu

（一）根据音频内容，选择正确答案 Choose the correct answers according to the recording.

（　　）1. 林一诺、杜无美和王成在哪里见面和谈话？
　　　A. 教室　　　　B. Facetime　　　C. 办公室　　　D. 微信
（　　）2. 杜无美刚刚在哪里吃了饭？
　　　A. 成都339　　B. 酒吧　　　　　C. 家里　　　　D. 餐厅
（　　）3. 王成认为抖音有什么缺点？
　　　A. 上面的内容很有意思　　　　B. 需要花钱
　　　C. 能了解多姿多彩的生活　　　D. 占用时间
（　　）4. 以下哪个应用程序没有在对话中提到？
　　　A. 微信　　　B. 飞书　　　　　C. 支付宝　　　D. 抖音

（二）讨论 Discussion

除对话中提到的应用程序，你还知道哪些中国应用软件？谈谈它们对你在中国的生活的影响。

Besides the online apps mentioned in the conversation, do you know any other Chinese apps? Please share your experience on how these apps influence your life in China.

任务三（Task Three）

看视频，完成练习 Watch the video and do the exercises.

赵丽川和何蓉蓉在家门口碰见了，她们聊起了自己的运动方式。

Zhao Lichuan and He Rongrong meet in front of the door, talking about their physical exercise.

生词和短语（New Words and Expressions）

1. 好巧	hǎo qiǎo	形	coincidental
2. 社区	shèqū	名	community
3. 公园	gōngyuán	名	park
4. 空地	kòngdì	名	open space

续表
Continued

5. 锻炼	duànliàn	动	to take exercise
6. 中老年人	zhōng-lǎonián rén	短	the middle-aged and old people
7. 年轻人	niánqīng rén	短	the young
8. 欢快	huānkuài	形	lively
9. 健康	jiànkāng	形	healthy
10. 流行歌曲	liúxíng gēqǔ	短	pop music and songs
11. 潮流	cháoliú	名	trend
12. 绿道	lǜdào	名	greenway
13. 跑步	pǎo bù	动	to run, to jog
14. 散步	sàn bù	动	to take a walk

（一）根据视频内容填空 Fill in the blanks according to the video.

赵丽川和妈妈在小区门口碰见了何蓉蓉，她们俩正要去_____。这是一种很多人一起跳的舞，可以在_____和_____跳，既放松心情，又锻炼身体。现在不仅有中老年人参与，越来越多的_____也喜欢这种运动方式，因为音乐中有很多_____，跟得上潮流，很欢快，又健康。何蓉蓉则是要去小区附近的_____跑步，每天有很多人在那里跑步、_____、_____。现在的人们运动方式越来越多了，生活也更加丰富了。

（二）讨论 Discussion

谈谈你自己国家特有的锻炼方式或舞蹈形式。
Please share your country's special ways of exercise or dances that you know.

（三）听音乐，尝试跳一段广场舞 Listen to the music and try a piece of square dance.

Unit 9 Contemporary Lifestyle in Chengdu

任务四（Task Four）

听录音，完成练习 Listen to the recording and do the exercises.

生词和短语（New Words and Expressions）

1. 乡村	xiāngcūn	名	countryside, village
2. 休闲娱乐	xiūxián yúlè	短	recreation and entertainment
3. 度假	dùjià	动	to vacation
4. 近郊	jìnjiāo	名	suburb
5. 愉悦精神	yúyuè jīngshén	短	to bring spiritual pleasure and joys
6. 发源地	fāyuándì	名	cradle, origin
7. 桃花	táohuā	名	peach blossom
8. 梨花	líhuā	名	pear flower
9. 油菜花	yóucàihuā	名	rape flower
10. 放风筝	fàng fēngzheng	短	kite flying
11. 晒太阳	shài tàiyáng	短	to sunbathe
12. 农家菜	nóngjiācài	名	farm food
13. 避暑	bì shǔ	动	to spend a holiday at a summer resort
14. 戏水	xì shuǐ	动	to play with/in water
15. 清凉	qīngliáng	形	cool
16. 天高气爽	tiāngāo qìshuǎng	短	the sky being high and the weather being fine
17. 瓜果飘香	guāguǒ piāoxiāng	短	mature fruits and vegetables with fragrance
18. 采摘	cǎizhāi	动	to pick
19. 农产品	nóngchǎnpǐn	名	farm product
20. 打麻将	dǎ májiàng	短	to play mahjong
21. 忙里偷闲	mánglǐ-tōuxián	成	to snatch a moment, to take time out of a busy schedule
22. 田园风光	tiányuán fēngguāng	短	rural scenery
23. 蔬菜瓜果	shūcài guāguǒ	短	fruits and vegetables

相遇天府
——中文视听说
Encountering Sichuan: Chinese Video-watching, Listening and Speaking

（一）根据录音内容，将左右适当内容连线 Match the activities with seasons according to the recording.

1. 春天　　　　A. 摆龙门阵、喝茶
2. 夏天　　　　B. 放风筝、赏百花
3. 秋冬　　　　C. 避暑、戏水

（二）口语练习 Speaking Practice

1. 为什么成都人喜欢"农家乐"？
2. 在"农家乐"里，人们一般都会做些什么活动？

📝 语法点注释（Grammar Notes）

现在越来越多年轻人也跳广场舞了，既好玩儿，又能锻炼身体。

"既……又/也/还……"是并列关联词，连接两个表示并列关系的分句。

"既……又/也/还……" are coordinating related words, connecting two clauses that indicate a parallel connection.

①现在越来越多年轻人也加入广场舞啦，既方便，又能锻炼身体。
②我们都喜欢和赵丽川交朋友，她既善良，还幽默。
③许多人都认为，成都的生活既安逸、舒适，还快捷、便利。

📝 扩展活动（Extended Activities）

去成都春熙路或者太古里了解更多当代成都人的生活方式，探究和体会现代中国发展趋势、时尚潮流。请你作为成都的城市推介人，以"中国的现当代""生活方式""经济""商业""潮流趋势"等为关键词，在班上做一个报告并进行讨论。

Please go to Chunxi Road or TaiKooLi in Chengdu to learn more about the contemporary lifestyles in Chengdu, and explore and experience the development trends and fashion trends of modern China. Then, acting as an introducer of

Chengdu city, do a presentation on this topic with modern and contemporary lifestyles, economy, business, trends, etc. as keywords.

文化小贴士（Cultural Tips）

生活方式对于一个人来说，具有双向影响：第一，它是人"社会化"的一项重要内容，生活方式决定了个体社会化的性质、水平和方向；第二，它是一个历史范畴，随着社会的发展而变化。不同社会、不同历史时期、不同阶层和不同职业的人构成了不同的生活方式，而生活方式的变化又直接或间接影响着一个人的思想意识和价值观念。

Lifestyle has a two-way impact on a person. Firstly, it is an important part of a person's "socialization". Lifestyle determines the nature, level and direction of individual socialization. Secondly, it is a historical category concept, which changes with the development of society. People from different societies, different historical periods, different classes and different occupations constitute different lifestyles. Changes in lifestyles directly or indirectly affect a person's ideology and values.

第十单元 多彩中国
Unit 10　Regional Differences in China

导入（Lead-in）

你去过中国哪些地方？这些地方有哪些差异？
Where have you been in China? Can you list some of their regional differences?

任务一（Task One）

看视频，完成练习 Watch the video and do the exercises.

Unit 10　Regional Differences in China

生词和短语（New Words and Expressions）

1.	陆地	lùdì	名	land
2.	面积	miànjī	名	area
3.	平方公里	píngfāng gōnglǐ	量	square kilometer
4.	平方	píngfāng	量	square
5.	公里	gōnglǐ	量	kilometer
6.	人口	rénkǒu	名	population
7.	亿	yì	数	100 million
8.	省	shěng	名	province
9.	自治区	zìzhìqū	名	autonomous region
10.	特别行政区	tèbié xíngzhèngqū	短	special administration zone
11.	行政	xíngzhèng	名	administration
12.	地理条件	dìlǐ tiáojiàn	短	geographical conditions
13.	条件	tiáojiàn	名	condition, environment
14.	沙漠	shāmò	名	desert
15.	其次	qícì	代	then, next
16.	饮食	yǐnshí	名	dieting
17.	再次	zàicì	副	thirdly; again
18.	少数民族	shǎoshù mínzú	短	ethnic minority
19.	少数	shǎoshù	名	minority
20.	民族	mínzú	名	ethnic group, nationality, people
21.	风俗习惯	fēngsú xíguàn	短	customs
22.	团结友爱	tuánjié yǒuài	短	solidarity and friendship
23.	家庭	jiātíng	名	family
24.	优点	yōudiǎn	名	merit, advantage

相遇天府
——中文视听说
Encountering Sichuan: Chinese Video-watching, Listening and Speaking

专有名词（Proper Names）

1. 贵州	Guìzhōu	Guizhou Province
2. 湖南	Húnán	Hunan Province
3. 江苏	Jiāngsū	Jiangsu Province
4. 浙江	Zhèjiāng	Zhejiang Province
5. 福建	Fújiàn	Fujian Province
6. 广东	Guǎngdōng	Guangdong Province

（一）根据视频内容，判断正误 Decide whether the following statements are true or false according to the video.

（　　）1. 中国面积大，人口多，但是各地差异比较小。
（　　）2. 各地的饮食习惯不一样。北方人喜欢吃面食，南方人喜欢吃米饭。
（　　）3. 中国各地方言差不多，写的时候都用汉字，人们也能互相听懂。
（　　）4. 中国一共有55个民族，汉族人口最多。
（　　）5. 中国的城市和农村差别比较大，人们都喜欢住在城市。

（二）根据视频内容填空 Fill in the blanks according to the video.

1. 中国陆地面积大约_____平方公里，人口一共_____多，有_____个省、5个自治区、_____个直辖市和2个特别行政区。

2. _____有很多高原，_____还有沙漠，中部和东部大平原_____。

3. 四川、贵州和湖南等地方的人喜欢吃_____，上海、江苏和浙江一带的人喜欢吃_____，广东、福建这些地方的人喜欢吃_____。

4. 北方方言和普通话_____，大家差不多能互相听懂；但是南方很多方言差别_____，人们互相听不懂。

5. 一般来说，城市的交通更_____，人更多，工作_____也多；农村生活压力更_____，空气更新鲜，也更_____一些。

任务二（Task Two）

听录音，完成练习 Listen to the recording and do the exercises.

何蓉蓉、王成和赵丽川在食堂聊南北差异。
He Rongrong, Wang Cheng and Zhao Lichuan are talking about the differences between the north and south of China in the canteen.

生词和短语（New Words and Expressions）

1. 差异	chāyì	名	difference
2. 算	suàn	动	(kind of) to be
3. 老家	lǎojiā	名	original hometown
4. 主食	zhǔshí	名	staple food
5. 面食	miànshí	名	wheat flour food
6. 怪不得	guài·bu·de	副	no wonder
7. 普通话	pǔtōnghuà	名	Mandarin Chinese
8. 下雪	xià xuě	动	to snow

专有名词（Proper Names）

巴基斯坦	Bājīsītǎn	Pakistan

（一）根据录音内容，判断正误 Decide whether the following statements are true or false according to the recording.

（   ）1. 王成和赵丽川都是南方人。
（   ）2. 四川属于南方。
（   ）3. 在北方也有人吃米饭，在四川也有人吃面食。
（   ）4. 对北方人来说，广东话和上海话比四川话更容易听懂。
（   ）5. 南方和北方的气候不一样。

（二）角色扮演 Role-play

四人一组，一人扮演一个角色，讨论中国南北方的差异，比如天气、饮食、方言等。

Four students form a group and each student plays one role. The theme is about the regional differences between the north and south of China, such as the weather, the food, and the dialect, etc.

任务三（Task Three）

看视频，完成练习 Watch a video and do the exercises.

林一诺、何蓉蓉和乔筝在教学楼走廊聊暑假旅游经历。

Lin Yinuo, He Rongrong and Qiao Zheng are chatting about their summer holiday travel experience at the classroom building corridor.

北京故宫博物院（The Palace Museum in Beijing）

Unit 10 Regional Differences in China

西昌彝族舞蹈（Yi People's Dance in Xichang）

生词和短语（New Words and Expressions）

1. 高铁	gāotiě	名	high-speed railway
2. 主要	zhǔyào	副	mainly
3. 当地	dāngdì	形	local
4. 展示	zhǎnshì	动	to display
5. 寒假	hánjià	名	winter holiday

专有名词（Proper Names）

1. 西昌	Xīchāng	Xichang, a city in Sichuan Province
2. 天安门广场	Tiān'ānmén Guǎngchǎng	Tian'anmen Square
3. 北京烤鸭	Běijīng Kǎoyā	Beijing Roast Duck
4. 凉山	Liángshān	Liangshan Yi Autonomous Prefecture in Sichuan
5. 彝族	Yízú	Yi People
6. 羌族	Qiāngzú	Qiang People
7. 苗族	Miáozú	Miao People

（一）根据视频内容，选择正确答案 Choose the correct answers according to the video.

（　　）1. 下面哪个地方，何蓉蓉和乔箺暑假在北京的时候没有去？
　　　　A. 故宫　　　　　　B. 长城
　　　　C. 天安门广场　　　D. 北京大学

（　　）2. 林一诺去了西昌哪些地方？
　　　　A. 邛海　　　　　　B. 凉山彝族博物馆
　　　　C. 青城山　　　　　D. A和B

（　　）3. 下列哪个不是西昌的特点？
　　　　A. 冬天很冷　　　　B. 自然风景很美
　　　　C. 少数民族多　　　D. 气候好

（　　）4. 关于北京和西昌的差异，下面哪个方面视频中没有提到？
　　　　A. 气候　　　　　　B. 景点
　　　　C. 民族　　　　　　D. 方言

（二）讨论 Discussion

你们国家有少数民族吗？这些少数民族有什么独特的文化？

Are there any ethnic minorities in your country? What unique cultures do they have?

任务四（Task Four）

听录音，完成练习 Listen to the recording and do the exercises.

杜无羡、赵丽川在饭店和老板聊中国的城市和农村。

Du Wuxian and Zhao Lichuan are chatting with the restaurant boss about China's urban and rural areas.

Unit 10　Regional Differences in China

第十单元　多彩中国

中国城市（A City in China）　　　中国农村（A Countryside in China）

生词和短语（New Words and Expressions）

1. 家常菜	jiāchángcài	名	homemade dish
2. 到处	dàochù	副	everywhere
3. 挨	āi	动	to be close to
4. 缩小	suōxiǎo	动	to reduce, to lessen, to narrow down
5. 赶快	gǎnkuài	副	hurriedly

专有名词（Proper Names）

| 村村通 | Cūncūntōng | Every Village Coverage, a national project to extend roads, electricity, tap water, radio, cable TV and the internet, etc. to every village |

（一）根据录音内容填空 Fill in the blanks according to the recording.

杜无美和赵丽川在钱老板的饭店吃饭，他们觉得这里的菜很好吃，也很有_____。原来，老板是四川农村来的，这些菜是他_____的家常菜，但是在城里很受欢迎。中国的城市和农村有一些不一样。比如，在农村，人没有这么多，但是成都这样的大城市里_____。还有，在农村，各家的房子一般离得_____；在城市，大家住在_____里，家家挨着。另外，农村因为人少车少，空气_____。最后，农村一般没有公共汽车，只有城市附近的农村才有，主要是因为_____。不过由于"村村通"工程，农村的

111

交通_____。现在中国正在建设美丽新农村，_____城市和农村的差别，以后农村_____。

（二）口语练习 Speaking Practice

1. 你们国家的城市和农村有什么差异？

Are there any differences between the city and the countryside in your country?

2. 你喜欢住在城市还是农村？为什么？

Where do you prefer to live, in the city or in the countryside? Why?

语法点注释（Grammar Notes）

1. 广东人听不懂上海话，上海人也听不懂广东话。

中文中一些在意义上能补充说明动作结果的形容词和动词可以用在动词谓语后面，表示动作的结果，这种补语叫作结果补语。动词和补语之间肯定形式用"得"，否定形式用"不"。

In Chinese, some adjectives and verbs can be put right after the verbal predicate, explaining the result of an action, which are called "Resultative Compliment". "得" is used between the verb and the compliment in the affirmative form, while "不"is used in the negative form.

①你听得懂四川话吗？

②我可能听不懂有些南方方言。

2. 我是从农村出来来成都的。

由两个或两个以上的动词充当谓语，或由连动短语直接构成的句子，叫"连动句"。在语义上有目的和方式、原因和结果、先和后的关系。

This structure consists of two or more than two verbs/verbal phrases serving as the predicate together, which is called "Coverbial Sentence". Semantically, they can indicate purpose and method, reason and result, or the sequential order.

①我们打的来吃这家北方菜。

②城里人到农村去度假，可是农村人到城市去旅游。

Unit 10　Regional Differences in China

扩展活动（Extended Activities）

问问你周边的朋友，或者假期亲自去调查一下中国东部和中西部地区的差异，例如自然地理、经济发展、人口、饮食、方言等，然后在班上做一个报告。

Interview your friends or do a survey in the holidays about the differences between the east and middle western regions in China, such as geographical conditions, economic development, population, food, and dialects, etc. And then do a presentation on this topic.

文化小贴士（Cultural Tips）

文化有广义和狭义的概念。狭义的文化指的是一个群体的人们一种共同的精神观念和行为习惯。这种共同的精神观念和行为习惯是这个环境中的人们由于地理环境、生活经验和历史传统相同而慢慢形成的，不是某个个体特有的。不同的群体、区域或国家的这种精神观念和行为习惯互有差异。中国有句俗语叫"一方水土养一方人"，不同的自然环境会对各地的文化和人的性格带来影响，从而形成地域文化差异。文化差异即是指因地区差别，以及各地区人们在行为和精神层面如观念、方言、风俗习惯、饮食等方面的不同而产生的差异。

Culture is a common behavioral and psychological procedure in a community or environment, formed gradually in this region by the local people who have common geographical environments, life experience, and historical traditions. It is a common procedure rather than an individual feature. And this procedure differs between different communities and regions. There is a proverb in China which goes that each place has its own way of supporting its own inhabitants. The geographic environment influences the local culture and personalities of the inhabitants living in this place, hence the formation of regional cultural differences. The cultural difference thus refers to the behavior and spiritual differences of the people such as beliefs, dialects, customs, and food, etc. caused by the regional differences.

附录1：练习参考答案
Appendix 1：Key to the Exercises

第一单元（Unit 1）

任务一（Task One）

(一)略

(二)1. ×　　2. √　　3. √　　4. √　　5. ×

(三)1. 高大　2. 环境　3. 宿舍楼　4. 公园　5. 春天　夏天　秋天

任务二（Task Two）

(一)1. ×　　2. ×　　3. ×　　4. √　　5. √

(二)1. A　　2. C　　3. C　　4. A　　5. C

(三)略 Open

任务三（Task Three）

(一)

1. 早晨在湖边散散步，看看天鹅，听听鸟叫。

2. 每年十一月，校园里的银杏叶都黄了，金灿灿的。

3. 银杏节就是我们学校为了"赏银杏美景，品传统文化"而举办的活动。

4. 校园里有各种各样的活动，比如，猜谜语、音乐会、健身运动什么的，还有摄影展和美食展。

5. 略 Open

6. 学校图书馆一楼的咖啡馆。

(二)略 Open

附录1：练习参考答案
Appendix 1：Key to the Exercises

任务四（Task Four）

（一）1. B   2. B C   3. A B C   4. A   5. C

（二）略 Open

扩展活动（Extended Activities）略 Open

第二单元（Unit 2）

任务一（Task One）

（一）1. √   2. ×   3. √   4. √   5. √   6. √   7. √

（二）

1. 西南部　中部　2. 大大小小　3. 名　开始　3000（三千）　开始
4. 大概　　　5. 叫作　　　6. 跟……有关

任务二（Task Two）

（一）1. ×   2. ×   3. ×   4. √   5. √   6. ×

（二）

机场　差不多/大概　很忙　休闲　越来越　轻松　堵车　堵车　心情
一点儿　蓉城　很多地方　不认识　有时间

（三）略 Open

任务三（Task Three）

（一）1. A   2. C   3. B   4. C   5. D

（二）

1. 一方面，因为有都江堰水利工程，成都平原不旱不涝，粮食充裕，物产丰富，就像天然的府库一样；另一方面，这里战争不多，人们生活得安定舒服，所以叫"天府之国"。

2. 据说"太阳神鸟"图案中间"太阳"的十二道阳光象征着十二个月，外边四只"神鸟"的图案象征着四个季节。

任务四（Task Four）

（一）略 Open

（二）略 Open

扩展活动（Extended Activities）略 Open

第三单元（Unit 3）

任务一（Task One）

（一）1.√　　2.×　　3.√　　4.×　　5.×

（二）

1.宜居　气候　　2.湿润　　3.主要枢纽机场　大多数城市　航班

4.地铁　公共汽车　二环高架快速公交车　　5.直接

任务二（Task Two）

（一）1. A　　2. A　　3.B　　4. C　　5. C

（二）略 Open

任务三（Task Three）

（一）1.√　　2.√　　3.×　　4.√　　5.√

（二）略 Open

（三）略 Open

任务四（Task Four）

（一）1.√　　2.√　　3.×　　4.√　　5.×

（二）略 Open

扩展活动（Extended Activities）略 Open

第四单元（Unit 4）

任务一（Task One）

（一）1. A   2. C   3. B   4. C   5. C

（二）略 Open

任务二（Task Two）

（一）

1. 没有去过。

2. 传统建筑、雕塑、楹联、绘画、音乐等。

3. 不用走很远的路。从他们那里去青羊宫，交通很方便。

4. 他想在手机上查去青羊宫的交通路线。他没有查，因为赵丽川把交通路线告诉了大家。

5.（1）在学校西门见面；

（2）一起出发，坐地铁2号线；

（3）在"青羊宫站"下来，出了站就到了。

（二）略 Open

任务三（Task Three）

（一）

1. 文殊院都环境真不错。因为游客一进来就感觉很清静。

2. 放慢脚步，放松心情，体验慢生活。

3. 文殊院在禅宗中的地位非常重要。

4. 文殊院现在的建筑是大约三百年前重修的。

5. 文殊院还有展览室，用来展览中国书法和绘画作品。

（二）

1. 环境　清静　2. 感兴趣　3. 脚步　心情　慢生活

4. 建筑　雕塑　书法　5. 重修

任务四（Task Four）

（一）1. ×　　2. √　　3. √　　4. √　　5. √

（二）略 Open

扩展活动（Extended Activities）略 Open

第五单元（Unit 5）

任务一（Task One）

（一）1. C　　2. B　　3. D　　4. C

（二）都江堰　青城山　乐山　峨眉山　九寨沟　黄龙　川南　川西

任务二（Task Two）

（一）
1. ×　2. ×　3. √　4. √　5. ×　6. √　7. √　8. ×

（二）乐山大佛　高大　尊　了不起　拜佛　运气　幸运
　　　神奇/奇妙　猴子　零食

任务三（Task Three）

（一）1. A　　2. C　　3. D　　4. A

（二）1. 壮观 五颜六色　2. 巨龙　3. 高原反应　4. 神话　5. 故宫 长城

任务四（Task Four）

（一）1. √　　2. √　　3. ×　　4. ×　　5. √

（二）

1. 因为机票贵，而且九寨沟离成都不远，不用坐飞机。

2. 他们不能坐高铁去九寨沟，因为成都到九寨沟没有高铁。

3. 她觉得参加旅行团不好玩。

4. 他们决定自己开车，去九寨沟自驾游。

5. 他们需要租一辆车,在网上预订好住的地方,买好保险,准备好相机。

扩展活动(Extended Activities)略 Open

第六单元（Unit 6）

任务一（Task One）

（一）

1. 就是开展一年内最大的室内清洁。

2. 就是穿着新衣服,带着茶叶、点心、酒等礼品到亲戚家里拜年。

3. 一方面是为了纪念李冰父子,他们二人在2200多年前带领大家修建都江堰水利工程,造福成都平原;另一方面也象征着一年春耕的开始,人们祈求五谷丰登、国泰民安。

4. 每年的9月1日。

5. 色彩丰富、风格独特。

（二）1. C   2. A   3. B   4. A

任务二（Task Two）

（一）1. B   2. D   3. A   4. D

（二）略 Open

任务三（Task Three）

（一）

1. 有红白喜事的时候。

2. 左邻右舍、亲朋好友。

3. 就是"大碗"的意思。

4. 穷人家只摆七碗。

（二）略 Open

任务四（Task Four）

（一）1. A   2. A.   3. D

（二）略 Open

扩展活动（Extended Activities）略 Open

第七单元 （Unit 7）

任务一 （Task One）

（一）1.√　　2.×　　3.×　　4.×　　5.√

（二）
1.四　闻名　2.百百　3.甜　4.很多　伤心　三　会　5.火锅

任务二 （Task Two）

（一）1.×　　2.√　　3.√　　4.×

（二）1. B　　2. D　　3. B　　4. D　　5. A

（三）needs boiling: 牛肉　土豆　　needs instant boiling: 肥牛　鸭肠　毛肚

任务三 （Task Three）

（一）1. e　　2. a　　3. c　　4. b　　5. d

（二）1.√　　2.×　　3.×　　4.√　　5.√

（三）1.宫保鸡丁 2.她也说不清楚

任务四 （Task Four）

（一）1.√　　2.×　　3.×

（二）1. 有关　家乡　特别　以为　　2. 以前　　3. 蔬菜　肉

扩展活动（Extended Activities）略 Open

第八单元 （Unit 8）

任务一 （Task One）

（一）1.×　　2.√　　3.×　　4.√　　5.√

附录1：练习参考答案
Appendix 1：Key to the Exercises

（二）

1. 原产地 故乡 饮茶制茶
2. 种植 制作 饮用
3. 大山 气候 地理环境
4. 掏耳朵 擦皮鞋 算命看相
5. 迷人的魅力 悠闲的生活

任务二（Task Two）

（一）1. √　　2. √　　3. ×　　4. √　　5. √

（二）略 Open

任务三（Task Three）

（一）1. C　　2. B　　3. D　　4. B

（二）略 Open

扩展活动（Extended Activities）略 Open

第九单元 （Unit 9）

任务一（Task One）

（一）1. ×　　2. √　　3. √　　4. ×

（二）1. D　　2. A　　3. B　　4. C

任务二（Task Two）

（一）1. D　　2. C　　3. D　　4. B

任务三（Task Three）

（一）跳广场舞　社区广场　公园空地　年轻人　流行歌曲　绿道　散步健身

（二）略 Open

任务四（Task Four）

（一）1—B，2—C，3—A

扩展活动(Extended Activities)略 Open

第十单元 （Unit 10）

任务一（Task One）

（一）1.×　　2.√　　3.×　　4.√　　5.×

（二）
1. 960　14亿　23　4
2. 西部　西北部　比较多
3. 辣的　甜的　清淡的
4. 比较像　比较大
5. 方便　机会　小　安静

任务二（Task Two）

（一）1.×　　2.√　　3.√　　4.×　　5.√

（二）略 Open

任务三（Task Three）

（一）1. D　　2. D　　3. A　　4. C

（二）略 Open

任务四（Task Four）

（一）特色　老家　到处都是人　比较远　楼房　比城市的新鲜　农村人口比较少　比以前方便多了　缩小　越来越好

（二）略 Open

扩展活动(Extended Activities)略 Open

附录2：词汇总表
Appendix 2：Vocabulary

生词和短语（New Words and Expressions）

A				
挨	āi	动	to be close to	10
矮桌	ǎi zhuō	短	low table	8
安定	āndìng	形	stable, settled	2
安逸	ānyì	形	easy and comfortable	9
B				
拜佛	bài fó	动	to worship Buddha	5
百听不厌	bǎitīng-búyàn	成	worth hearing a hundred times	1
摆放	bǎifàng	动	to put in order	1
拜年	bài nián	动	to give Chinese New Year greetings, to pay a Chinese New Year visit	6
班车	bānchē	名	regular bus	5
伴奏	bànzòu	动	to accompany with musical instruments	6
保险	bǎoxiǎn	名	insurance	5
巴适	bāshi	形	a word in Sichuan dialect with the meaning of "comfortable" or "feeling good"	6
杯沿	bēiyán	名	rim of a cup	8
扁担	biǎndan	名	carrying or shoulder pole	7
便利	biànlì	形	convenient	1
表达	biǎodá	动	to convey, to express	2

123

续表
Continued

表演	biǎoyǎn	动	to perform	4
冰川	bīngchuān	名	glacier	5
避暑	bì shǔ	动	to spend a holiday at a summer resort	9
不停	bùtíng	副	ceaselessly, constantly	5
不错	búcuò	形	not bad	9
C				
菜系	càixì	名	style of cooking	7
采摘	cǎizhāi	动	to pick	9
蚕	cán	名	silk worm	2
灿烂	cànlàn	形	bright, magnificent	1
茶单	chádān	名	tea menu	8
茶盖	chágài	名	tea lid	8
茶礼	chálǐ	名	tea etiquette	8
茶碗	cháwǎn	名	tea bowl	8
差别	chābié	名	difference	8
差不多	chà·buduō	副	almost	1
茶馆	cháguǎn	名	teahouse	6
茶具	chájù	名	tea set	8
产地	chǎndì	名	place of production	8
场地	chǎngdì	名	venue, yard	8
场面	chǎngmiàn	名	occasion, scene	6
唱腔	chàngqiāng	名	singing tunes in Chinese operas	6
场所	chǎngsuǒ	名	site, place	2
禅宗	chánzōng	名	the Zen sect (of Buddhism)	4
炒	chǎo	动	to stir-fry	7
潮流	cháoliú	名	trend	9

附录2：词汇总表
Appendix 2: Vocabulary

续表
Continued

潮湿	cháoshī	形	humid	7
差异	chāyì	名	difference	10
丞相	chéngxiàng	名	premier (of ancient China)	4
驰名中外	chímíng-zhōngwài	成	famous and popular at home and abroad	6
崇拜	chóngbài	名、动	worship; to worship	2
充实	chōngshí	形	rich, plentiful, full	1
重修	chóngxiū	动	to rebuild	4
充裕	chōngyù	形	abundant, plentiful	2
串串	chuànchuan	名	clusters: a kind of spicy hot snack	7
创业	chuàngyè	动	to start businesses	9
传说	chuánshuō	名	legend, tale	5
传统	chuántǒng	名	tradition	1
出汗	chūhàn	动	to sweat	7
除了	chúle	介	besides, except	1
纯	chún	形	pure	7
春耕	chūngēng	名	spring ploughing	6
刺	cì	名	bone (of the fish)	7
匆忙	cōngmáng	形	hasty	4
D				
大街小巷	dàjiē-xiǎoxiàng	成	high streets and back lanes	2
打麻将	dǎ májiàng	动	to play mahjong	9
打盹儿	dǎ dǔnr	动	to take a nap	8
代表	dàibiǎo	名	representative	7
单车	dānchē	名	bike	3
当地	dāngdì	形	local	10

续表
Continued

当地人	dāngdì rén	短	local people	5
大年	dànián	名	the Spring Festival	6
淡绿	dànlǜ	形	light green	8
担心	dān xīn	动	to worry about	7
到处	dàochù	副	everywhere	10
到底	dàodǐ	副	on earth	5
道教	Dàojiào	名	Taoism, Daoism	4
导师	dǎoshī	名	supervisor	1
导游	dǎoyóu	名	tour guide	5
大小	dàxiǎo	名	size	8
大型	dàxíng	形	large, large-scale	1
大熊猫	dàxióngmāo	名	giant panda	4
打坐	dǎzuò	动	to sit in meditation	4
等不及	děng·bují	短	can't wait	5
等级	děngjí	名	grade, class	8
典型	diǎnxíng	形	typical	4
电子产品	diànzǐ chǎnpǐn	短	electronic product	9
电子显示屏	diànzǐ xiǎnshìpíng	短	electronic screen	3
雕刻	diāokè	动	to carve	5
雕塑	diāosù	名	sculpture	2
地理	dìlǐ	名	geography	2
地理条件	dìlǐ tiáojiàn	短	geographical conditions	10
定	dìng	动	to decide	4
地区	dìqū	名	area, region	2
的确	díquè	副	indeed	2
地势	dìshì	名	terrain, topography	2

附录2：词汇总表
Appendix 2: Vocabulary

续表
Continued

动作	dòngzuò	名	action	8
断	duàn	动	to stop, to cut off	2
锻炼	duànliàn	动	to take exercise	9
堵车	dǔ chē	动	to get stuch in a traffic jam	2
都城	dūchéng	名	capital	2
度假	dùjià	动	to vacation	9
顿	dùn	量	for times of meals or beating	6
炖	dùn	动	to stew	7
多姿多彩	duōzī duōcǎi	短	colorful and varied	9
独特	dútè	形	unique	4
F				
发达	fādá	形	developed, advanced	2
发明	fāmíng	名	invention	2
发明	fāmíng	动	to invent	7
翻	fān	动	to turn over	8
放风筝	fàng fēngzheng	短	kite flying	9
放松	fàngsōng	动	to relax	1
方言	fāngyán	名	dialect, vernacular	6
繁华	fánhuá	形	prosperous, booming	4
翻译	fānyì	动	to translate	4
发现	fāxiàn	动	to discover	2
发源地	fāyuándì	名	cradle, origin	9
肥牛	féiniú	名	beef slides	7
丰富	fēngfù	形	abundant, rich	1
风格	fēnggé	名	style	4
风俗习惯	fēngsú xíguàn	短	customs	10

续表
Continued

分享	fēnxiǎng	动	to share	9
佛教	Fójiào	名	Buddhism	4
付	fù	动	to pay (money)	2
符号	fúhào	名	symbol, mark	4
府库	fǔkù	名	government treasury	2
芙蓉花	fúrónghuā	名	hibiscus	2
复杂	fùzá	形	complicated	4
富足	fùzú	形	abundant, plentiful	2
G				
改天	gǎitiān	副	some other day	2
赶	gǎn	动	to hurry through	3
感兴趣	gǎnxìngqù	短	to be interested in	1
赶快	gǎnkuài	副	hurriedly	10
高腔	gāoqiāng	名	a kind of rhyme scheme of Chinese operas	6
高人	gāorén	名	person of superior ability or accomplishment	4
高铁	gāotiě	名	high-speed railway	10
高原	gāoyuán	名	plateau	5
高原反应	gāoyuán fǎnyìng	短	altitude sickness	5
共享	gòngxiǎng	动、形	to share; shared	3
宫观	gōngguàn	名	(Taoist) temple and palace	4
公里	gōnglǐ	量	kilometer	10
工艺品	gōngyìpǐn	名	handicraft, artifact	4
公园	gōngyuán	名	park	9
购物中心	gòuwù zhōngxīn	短	shopping mall	1
古	gǔ	形	ancient, age-old	2

附录2：词汇总表
Appendix 2: Vocabulary

续表
Continued

瓜果飘香	guāguǒ piāoxiāng	短	mature fruits and vegetables with fragrance	9
怪不得	guài·bu·de	副	no wonder	10
广场	guǎngchǎng	名	square, plaza	1
广场舞	guǎngchǎngwǔ	名	square dance	9
广泛	guǎngfàn	形	extensive	7
光环	guānghuán	名	a circle of light, halo	5
逛街	guàng jiē	动	to go shopping, to stroll on the street	1
观众	guānzhòng	名	audience	6
归来	guīlái	动	to return	5
国宝	guóbǎo	名	national treasure	4
锅底	guōdǐ	名	hotpot seasoning	7
国际	guójì	名、形	world; international	2
国泰民安	guótài-mín'ān	成	contented people living in a country at peace	6
故乡	gùxiāng	名	hometown	7
H				
海拔	hǎibá	名	altitude	5
旱	hàn	名	drought	2
航班	hángbān	名	flight	3
航站楼	hángzhànlóu	名	terminal	3
寒假	hánjià	名	winter holiday	10
寒气	hánqì	名	coldness	7
好巧	hǎo qiǎo	形	coincidental	9
好像	hǎoxiàng	副	seemingly	7
河流	héliú	名	river	2
河鲜	héxiān	名	delicacy from rivers	7
红白喜事	hóng bái xǐshì	短	weddings and funerals	6

129

续表
Continued

花茶	huāchá	名	flower tea	1
皇帝	huángdì	名	emperor	2
环境	huánjìng	名	environment	4
欢快	huānkuài	形	lively	9
环形	huánxíng	形	ring-shaped, circular	5
欢迎	huānyíng	动	to welcome	7
绘画	huìhuà	名	painting	4
浑	hún	形	turbid	7
火锅	huǒguō	名	hotpot	7
J				
酒吧	jiǔbā	名	bar	9
记	jì	动	to write, to note	8
既……又……	jì...yòu...	连	both...and...	4
假	jiǎ	形	fake	2
家常菜	jiāchángcài	名	homemade dish	10
讲究	jiǎngjiu	动、形、名	to be particular about, to stress; posh; rules of etiquette	6
将军	jiāngjūn	名	general	2
健康	jiànkāng	形	healthy	9
建设	jiànshè	动	to build, to develop	2
健身	jiànshēn	动	to go to the gym, to work out	1
简直	jiǎnzhí	副	simply, just, virtually	5
建筑	jiànzhù	名	architecture	4
脚步	jiǎobù	名	footstep	4
叫法	jiàofǎ	名	way of naming a thing	5
郊区	jiāoqū	名	suburb	9
家庭	jiātíng	名	family	10

附录2：词汇总表
Appendix 2: Vocabulary

续表
Continued

家乡	jiāxiāng	名	hometown	7
驾照	jiàzhào	名	driver's license	5
基本	jīběn	形	basic	7
基地	jīdì	名	base	4
接触	jiēchù	动	to get in touch	4
街道	jiēdào	名	street, road	2
介绍	jièshào	动	to introduce	7
节奏	jiézòu	名	tempo	9
锦	jǐn	名	brocade	2
金灿灿	jīncàncàn	形	golden	1
景点	jǐngdiǎn	名	scenic spot	2
景观	jǐngguān	名	scenery, landscape	4
京剧	jīngjù	名	Beijing Opera, Peking Opera	6
静坐	jìngzuò	动	to sit quietly and meditate	4
金黄	jīnhuáng	形	golden yellow	1
纪念	jìniàn	动	to commemorate, to remember	2
近郊	jìnjiāo	名	inner suburb	9
巨龙	jùlóng	名	giant dragon	5
举办	jǔbàn	动	to run, to conduct, to hold	1
角色	juésè	名	role, part	6
距离	jùlí	名	distance	9
军事	jūnshì	名	military	2
均匀	jūnyún	形	even, uniform	8
据说	jùshuō	动	it is said that...	2
具有	jùyǒu	动	to possess, to have	6
居住	jūzhù	动	to live, to dwell	2

131

续表
Continued

K				
开启	kāiqǐ	动	to open, to unlock	1
看来	kànlái	动	to appear	7
看起来	kànqǐlái	短	seemingly	2
看相	kàn xiàng	动	to physiognomize	8
可爱	kě'ài	形	cute	1
磕头	kē tóu	动	to kowtow	6
客运站	kèyùnzhàn	名	passenger station	5
空地	kòngdì	名	open space	9
口感	kǒugǎn	名	flavor	7
快捷	kuàijié	形	easy and fast	9
困难	kùnnán	形	difficult	1
L				
辣	là	形	spicy	7
涝	lào	名	flood, waterlogging	2
老家	lǎojiā	名	original hometown	10
凉粉	liángfěn	名	bean jelly	7
粮食	liáng·shi	名	food, foodstuff	2
脸谱	liǎnpǔ	名	facial makeup in traditional Chinese operas	6
联系	liánxì	动	to contact	1
了不起	liǎo·buqǐ	形	amazing, terrific, extraordinary	5
梨花	líhuā	名	pear flower	9
零食	língshí	名	snack	5
历史	lìshǐ	名	history	2
历史悠久	lìshǐ yōujiǔ	短	time-honored, to have a long history	2

附录2：词汇总表
Appendix 2：Vocabulary

续表
Continued

流行歌曲	liúxíng gēqǔ	短	pop music and songs	9
流连忘返	liúlián-wàngfǎn	成	to enjoy oneself so much as to forget to go back	5
留下	liúxià	动	to leave behind	2
流行	liúxíng	动	to prevail, to be popular	6
礼物	lǐwù	名	gift, present	8
绿树成荫	lǜshù chéngyīn	短	green trees make a pleasant shade	1
绿道	lǜdào	名	greenway	9
旅游团	lǚyóutuán	名	tour	5
露天	lùtiān	副	outdoors	8
陆地	lùdì	名	land	10
M				
麻	má	形	tongue-numbing	7
麻烦	máfan	形	troublesome	7
忙里偷闲	mánglǐ-tōuxián	成	to snatch a moment, to take time out of a busy schedule	9
冒菜	màocài	名	instant spicy steampot	7
毛肚	máodǔ	名	tripe	7
美景	měijǐng	名	beautiful scenery	1
美丽	měilì	形	beautiful	1
魅力	mèilì	名	charm	8
美食街	měishíjiē	名	food street	1
美食展	měishízhǎn	名	food show	1
梦想	mèngxiǎng	名	dream	1
迷人	mírén	形	charming, enchanting	8
面积	miànjī	名	area	10
面具	miànjù	名	facial mask	6

133

续表
Continued

面食	miànshí	名	wheat flour food	10
庙	miào	名	temple, memorial temple	2
名称	míngchēng	名	name (of an object or organization)	2
名片	míngpiàn	名	name card, business card	7
名胜古迹	míngshèng gǔjì	短	scenic spots and historic places	2
冥想	míngxiǎng	动	to meditate	4
民俗	mínsú	名	folk customs	4
民族	mínzú	名	ethinc group, nationality, people	10
迷人	mírén	形	fascinating, charming	5
谜语	míyǔ	名	riddle	1
茉莉	mò·lì	名	jasmine	1
目的	mùdì	名	objective, purpose	4
N				
难为	nán·wei	动	to make it difficult, to be taxing	4
年轻人	niánqīng rén	短	the young	9
牛杂	niúzá	名	essence of beef offal	7
农产品	nóngchǎnpǐn	名	farm product	9
弄懂	nòngdǒng	动	to understand	4
农家菜	nóngjiācài	名	farm food	9
农家乐	nóngjiālè	名	agritainment, countryside recreation	9
农业	nóngyè	名	agriculture, farming	2
P				
牌子	páizi	名	sign	3
跑步	pǎo bù	动	to run, to jog	9
陪伴	péibàn	动	to accompany	1
盆地	péndì	名	basin	2

附录2：词汇总表
Appendix 2：Vocabulary

续表
Continued

烹饪	pēngrèn	动	to cook	7
碰头	pèng tóu	动	to meet	4
朋友圈	péngyouquān	名	moments（usu. in WeChat）	1
皮肤	pífū	名	skin	3
票价	piàojià	名	price of a ticket	5
品	pǐn	动	to sample, to taste	8
平放	píngfàng	动	to lay... flat	8
平民	píngmín	名	the common people	8
平方	píngfāng	量	square	10
平方公里	píngfāng gōnglǐ	量	square kilometer	10
平和	pínghé	形	peaceful	9
平坦	píngtǎn	形	flat, smooth	2
平原	píngyuán	名	plain	2
品质	pǐnzhì	名	quality	8
瀑布	pùbù	名	waterfall	5
菩萨	púsà	名	Bodhisattva（second only to Buddha）	4
普通话	pǔtōnghuà	名	Mandarin Chinese	10
Q				
起伏	qǐfú	动、形	to rise and fall; ups and downs	8
其次	qícì	代	then, next	10
旗杆	qígān	名	flagpole, flag post	1
奇怪	qíguài	形	weird, strange	7
气候	qìhòu	名	climate, weather	3
清楚	qīng·chu	形	clear	7
请教	qǐngjiào	动	to consult, to seek advice	8
清洁	qīngjié	名	cleaning	6

135

续表
Continued

清静	qīngjìng	形	quiet and sobering	4
清凉	qīngliáng	形	cool	9
轻松	qīngsōng	形	relaxed	2
亲朋好友	qīnpéng hǎoyǒu	短	relatives and friends	6
亲戚	qīn·qi	名	relative	6
气派	qìpài	名	style, grandeur	4
祈求	qíqiú	动	to pray for	6
气质	qìzhì	名	temperament	9
其中	qízhōng	名	among (which, them, etc.)	7
确实	quèshí	副	indeed	1
区域	qūyù	名	region	4
R				
人山人海	rénshān-rénhǎi	成	a sea of people, crowded conditions	3
热闹	rènao	形	lively, joyful	1
人口	rénkǒu	名	population	10
人文	rénwén	名	humanity	4
人物	rénwù	名	personage, person, figure	2
容易	róngyì	形	likely	7
S				
三吹三浪	sānchuī sānlàng	短	to make the lid of the bowl sumerged in the water and push it three times and then drink the tea in three times	8
散步	sàn bù	动	to take a walk	9
晒	shài	动	to bask	8
晒太阳	shài tàiyáng	短	to sunbathe	9
沙漠	shāmò	名	desert	10
伤心	shāngxīn	形	heart-broken	7

附录2：词汇总表
Appendix 2: Vocabulary

续表
Continued

商业模式	shāngyè móshì	短	business model	9
山珍	shānzhēn	名	delicacy from mountains	7
稍	shāo	副	slightly, a bit	5
烧	shāo	动	to braise	7
少数	shǎoshù	名	minority	10
少数民族	shǎoshù mínzú	短	ethnic minority	10
稍微	shāowēi	副	a little	7
省	shěng	名	province	10
声调	shēngdiào	名	tones (of Chinese characters)	2
省会	shěnghuì	名	provincial capital	2
生活	shēnghuó	名、动	life; to live	1
生机勃勃	shēngjī-bóbó	成	vivifying	2
深厚	shēnhòu	形	profound	2
神话	shénhuà	名	mythology, myth	5
神奇	shénqí	形	magical, miraculous, mystical	5
神仙	shénxiān	名	immortal, fairy	5
甚至	shènzhì	副	even, indeed	8
社区	shèqū	名	community	9
摄影展	shèyǐngzhǎn	名	photographic exhibition	1
适合	shìhé	动	to fit, to suit	8
湿润	shīrùn	形	wet, humid	3
失败	shībài	名、动	failure; to fail	2
食材	shícái	名	ingredient, food material	6
湿地公园	shīdì gōngyuán	短	wetland park	1
实际上	shíjì·shàng	副	in fact	7
视频	shìpín	名	video	9

续表
Continued

湿气	shīqì	名	moisture	7
实验室	shíyànshì	名	laboratory	1
使用	shǐyòng	动	to use, to employ	2
始祖	shǐzǔ	名	earliest ancestor	6
受	shòu	动	to receive, to accept	7
数	shǔ	动	to count	8
蔬菜瓜果	shūcài guāguǒ	短	fruits and vegetables	9
枢纽	shūniǔ	名	hub	3
水利	shuǐlì	名	water conservancy, irrigation works	6
水利工程	shuǐlì gōngchéng	短	water conservancy project, irrigation works, irrigation system	5
暑假	shǔjià	名	summer holiday	5
说法	shuōfǎ	名	way of saying	5
舒适	shūshì	形	comfortable	1
四面八方	sìmiàn-bāfāng	成	all directions	5
寺庙	sìmiào	名	temple	4
思念	sīniàn	动	to miss	7
寺院	sìyuàn	名	(Buddhist)monastery	4
算	suàn	动	(kind of)to be	10
酸	suān	形	sour	7
算了	suànle	动	to forget it, to just stop at that, to let it go at that	4
算命	suàn mìng	动	to tell fortune	8
俗话说	súhuà shuō	短	as the saying goes	8
碎	suì	形	fragmentary, full of bits	8
缩小	suōxiǎo	动	to reduce, to lessen, to narrow down	10
塑像	sùxiàng	名	sculpted statue	4

附录2：词汇总表
Appendix 2：Vocabulary

续表
Continued

塑造	sùzào	动	to mould	4
T				
烫	tàng	动	to boil food briefly	7
掏耳朵	tāo ěrduō	动	to pick the ears	8
桃花	táohuā	名	peach blossom	9
特别	tèbié	副	especially	7
特别行政区	tèbié xíngzhèngqū	短	special administration zone	10
特点	tèdiǎn	名	characteristics	7
特级	tèjí	形	extra grade, superfine	8
特色	tèsè	名	feature	4
甜	tián	形	sweet	7
天高气爽	tiāngāo qìshuǎng	短	the sky being high and the weather being fine	9
天鹅	tiān'é	名	swan	1
天然	tiānrán	形	natural	2
天下	tiānxià	名	land under heaven	5
田园风光	tiányuán fēngguāng	短	rural scenery	9
挑	tiāo	动	to carry	7
条件	tiáojiàn	名	condition, environment	10
调料	tiáoliào	名	seasoning, condiment	7
挺	tǐng	副	rather	7
听起来	tīngqǐlái	短	to sound	2
提前	tíqián	动	to do something in advance or ahead of time	5
体现	tǐxiàn	动	to embody	8
体验	tǐyàn	名、动	experience; to experience	3
通车	tōng chē	动	to be open to traffic	3

续表
Continued

通道	tōngdào	名	passageway	1
童话	tónghuà	名	fairy tale	5
投币	tóu bì	短	to insert coins	3
图案	tú'àn	名	pattern, design	2
团结友爱	tuánjié yǒuài	短	solidarity and friendship	10
推荐	tuījiàn	动	to recommend	4
W				
外卖	wàimài	名	takeaway food	9
网络	wǎngluò	名	network	9
网站	wǎngzhàn	名	website	9
味道	wèidào	名	taste	7
文化	wénhuà	名	culture	2
闻名	wénmíng	形	famous	7
温暖	wēnnuǎn	形	warm	1
问题	wèntí	名	problem	7
五彩斑斓	wǔcǎi-bānlán	成	multicolored and bright-colored	5
五颜六色	wǔyán-liùsè	成	colorful	5
物产	wùchǎn	名	product	2
五谷丰登	wǔgǔ-fēngdēng	成	an abundant harvest of all crops	6
武术	wǔshù	名	martial art	4
五香	wǔxiāng	名	the five kinds of seasoning: fennel, zanthoxylum, aniseed, cinnamon, clove	7
X				
下雪	xià xuě	动	to snow	10
峡谷	xiágǔ	名	gorge, canyon	5
咸	xián	形	salty	7

附录2：词汇总表
Appendix 2：Vocabulary

续表
Continued

鲜	xiān	形	fresh	8
闲书	xiánshū	名	light reading	8
馅儿	xiànr	名	stuffing	7
乡村	xiāngcūn	名	village	9
相机	xiàngjī	名	camera	5
想象	xiǎngxiàng	动	to imagine	5
相因	xiāngyīn	形	a word in Sichuan dialect with the meaning of "cheap"	6
象征	xiàngzhēng	名、动	symbol; to symbolize	2
现金	xiànjīn	名	cash	2
先进	xiānjìn	形	advanced	3
消费	xiāofèi	动	to consume	8
小吃	xiǎochī	名	snack	7
习惯	xíguàn	动	to be accustomed to	1
西南	xīnán	名	southwest	2
腥味	xīngwèi	名	fishy smell	7
幸运	xìngyùn	形	lucky	5
行政	xíngzhèng	名	administration	10
心情	xīnqíng	名	mood, state of mind	2
欣赏	xīnshǎng	动	to enjoy, to appriciate	5
新鲜	xīnxiān	形	fresh	9
戏曲	xìqǔ	名	traditional Chinese opera	6
戏水	xì shuǐ	动	to play with/in water	9
秀	xiù	形	beautiful, elegant, graceful	5
绣	xiù	名	embroidery	6
修	xiū	动	to build, to construct	2
修建	xiūjiàn	动	to build, to construct	4

141

续表
Continued

休闲	xiūxián	形	leisurely	2
休闲娱乐	xiūxiányúlè	短	recreation and entertainment	9
选修课	xuǎnxiūkè	名	elective course, optional course	1
选择	xuǎnzé	动	to choose, to select	5
需要	xūyào	动	to need	7
Y				
鸭肠	yācháng	名	duck intestine	7
养	yǎng	动	to raise, to grow, to keep	2
扬尘	yángchén	名	flying or hanging dust	6
阳光	yángguāng	名	sunlight	2
宴席	yànxí	名	banquet, feast	6
演员	yǎnyuán	名	actor, actress	6
野生	yěshēng	形	wild	8
亿	yì	数	100 million	10
宜居	yíjū	形	livable, suitable for living	3
一般	yìbān	副	commonly, usually	1
遗憾	yíhàn	动	to regret	5
宜居城市	yíjū chéngshì	短	livable city	2
移民	yímín	名、动	immigrant; to migrate	7
楹联	yínglián	名	couplet written on scrolls and hung on pillars	4
应用程序	yìngyòng chéngxù	短	application	9
饮食	yǐnshí	名	diet	10
以为	yǐwéi	动	to think, to believe	7
拥有	yōngyǒu	动	to possess, to have	4
油菜花	yóucàihuā	名	rape flowers	9
优点	yōudiǎn	名	merit, advantage	10

附录2：词汇总表
Appendix 2: Vocabulary

续表
Continued

有关	yǒuguān	动	to concern, to have something to do with	7
有关	yǒuguān	形	related to	1
有轨电车	yǒuguǐ diànchē	短	tramcar, trolley	3
悠久	yōujiǔ	形	time-honored, long-standing	2
优美	yōuměi	形	graceful, beautiful	5
幽默	yōumò	形	humorous	2
悠闲	yōuxián	形	leisurely, laidback, easygoing	8
优雅	yōuyǎ	形	elegant, graceful	1
由于	yóuyú	介	owing to, because of	6
原来	yuánlái	副	actually, originally	7
遇到	yùdào	动	to encounter	7
预订	yùdìng	动	to book, to reserve	5
越来越	yuèláiyuè	短	increasingly	2
乐器	yuèqì	名	musical instrument	6
玉佛	yùfó	名	jade Buddha	4
娱乐	yúlè	名	entertainment	1
运气	yùn·qi	名	luck	5
鱼香	yúxiāng	名	a taste made from pickled chili, onions, ginger, sugar, salt, etc.	7
愉悦精神	yúyuè jīngshén	短	to bring spiritual pleasure and joys	9
Z				
再次	zàicì	副	thirdly, again	10
在线视频	zàixiàn shìpín	短	online video call	9
暂时	zànshí	形	temporary	8
造福	zàofú	动	to bring benefit to	6
噪声	zàoshēng	名	noise	4

143

续表
Continued

沾	zhān	动	to stick to	7
长辈	zhǎngbèi	名	the senior people, elder member of a family	6
展览	zhǎnlǎn	动	to exhibit	4
展示	zhǎnshì	动	to display	10
占用	zhànyòng	动	to occupy	9
战争	zhànzhēng	名	war, warfare	2
著名	zhùmíng	形	famous	8
蒸	zhēng	形	steamed (dishes)	6
整齐	zhěngqí	形	neat, in good order	1
政治	zhèngzhì	名	politics	2
政治家	zhèngzhìjiā	名	statesman	4
纸	zhǐ	名	paper	2
织	zhī	动	to weave, to knit	2
至少	zhìshǎo	副	at least	7
制作	zhìzuò	动	to make	7
终点站	zhōngdiǎnzhàn	名	destination	3
中华	Zhōnghuá	名	(formal and literary) China	4
中老年人	zhōng-lǎonián rén	短	the middle aged and old people	9
中心	zhōngxīn	名	centre	1
种植	zhòngzhí	动	to plant	8
煮	zhǔ	动	to boil	7
竹叶	zhúyè	名	bamboo leaf	8
壮观	zhuàngguān	形	spectacular, magnificent	5
专业课	zhuānyèkè	名	professional course, major course	1
追求	zhuīqiú	动	pursue, aspire	1
准备	zhǔnbèi	动	to prepare	7

附录2：词汇总表
Appendix 2: Vocabulary

续表
Continued

主食	zhǔshí	名	staple food	10
主要	zhǔyào	副	mainly	10
竹子	zhúzi	名	bamboo	4
自驾游	zìjiàyóu	动	self-driving tour, road trip	5
资料	zīliào	名	material	1
自在	zìzai	形	free, at ease	8
自治区	zìzhìqū	名	autonomous region	10
宗教	zōngjiào	名	religion	4
组合	zǔhé	名、动	combination; to combine	7
尊	zūn	量	indicating a unit or a piece of sculpture	4
左邻右舍	zuǒlín-yòushè	成	neighbor	6
作为	zuòwéi	介	as	7
组织	zǔzhī	动	to organize	1

145

专有名词 (Proper Names)

A			
阿坝州	Ābà Zhōu	Aba Tibetan and Qiang Autonomous Prefecture	5
B			
巴基斯坦	Bājīsītǎn	Pakistan	10
坝坝宴	Bà·bayàn	banquet in the courtyard	6
北京烤鸭	Běijīng Kǎoyā	Beijing Roast Duck	10
钵钵鸡	Bōbō Jī	Bobo Chicken	7
C			
长城	Chángchéng	the Great Wall	5
成都339	Chéngdū Sānsānjiǔ	Chengdu 339, a bar zone in Chengdu	9
成都西站	Chéngdūxī Zhàn	Chengdu West Station	3
成华区	Chénghuá Qū	Chenghua District, a district of Chengdu City	2
重庆	Chóngqìng	Chongqing City, a municipality in southwest China	6
春熙路	Chūnxī Lù	Chunxi Road, a prosperous commercial street in Chengdu City	
村村通	Cūncūntōng	Every Village Coverage, a national project to extend roads, electricity, tap water, radio, cable TV and the internet, etc. to every village	10
D			
担担面	Dàndan Miàn	Dan Dan Noodles	7
蛋烘糕	Dàn Hōng Gāo	Baked Egg Cake	7
滴滴	Dīdī	Didi App, a shared taxi app	9
东湖	Dōnghú	East Lake	1
都江堰	Dūjiāngyàn	Dujiangyan City, a county-level city of Chengdu City	6
都江堰水利工程	Dūjiāngyàn Shuǐlì Gōngchéng	the Dujiangyan Water Conservancy Project	2

146

附录2：词汇总表
Appendix 2: Vocabulary

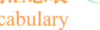

续表
Continued

抖音	Dǒuyīn	Chinese TikTok	9
杜甫	Dù Fǔ	Du Fu, a famous poet in the Tang dynasty	3
E			
峨眉毛峰	Éméi Máofēng	a green tea produced in Emei Mountain	8
峨眉山	Éméi Shān	Mount Emei	5
峨眉竹叶青	Éméi Zhúyèqīng	a green tea produced in Emei Mountain	8
F			
夫妻肺片	Fūqī Fèipiàn	Sliced Beef and Ox Tongue in Chili Sauce	7
福建	Fújiàn	Fujian Province	10
府河	Fǔhé	Fuhe River	2
G			
高新区	Gāoxīn Qū	Shortform of Hi-tech Industrial Development Zone, a district of Chengdu City	2
宫保鸡丁	Gōngbǎo Jīdīng	Diced Chicken with Paprika	7
故宫	Gùgōng	the Imperial Palace, the Forbidden City	5
怪味鸡	Guàiwèi Jī	Special Flavored Shredded Chicken	7
关羽	Guān Yǔ	Guan Yu (?-220), a general serving under the warlord Liu Bei	2
广东	Guǎngdōng	Guangdong Province	10
贵州	Guìzhōu	Guizhou Province	10
国家5A级旅游景区	Guójiā Wǔ'ēi Jí Lǚyóu Jǐngqū	Five A National Tourist Attraction	5
H			
合江亭	Héjiāng Tíng	Hejiang Pavilion	2
湖南	Húnán	Hunan Province	10
黄龙	Huánglóng	Huanglong Scenic and Historic Interest Area	5
回锅肉	Huíguō Ròu	Double-fried Pork Slices	7

续表
Continued

J			
夹江	Jiājiāng	Jiajiang County, a county in Sichuan Province	6
江苏	Jiāngsū	Jiangsu Province	10
江油	Jiāngyóu	Jiangyou City, a city in Sichuan Province	5
交子大道	Jiāozǐ Dàdào	Jiaozi Avenue	2
金沙遗址	Jīnshā Yízhǐ	Jinsha Relics, a historical relic of ancient Shu culture	2
锦江区	Jǐnjiāng Qū	Jinjiang District, a district of Chengdu City	2
京东	Jīngdōng	Jingdong, an online shopping mall	9
九眼桥	Jiǔyǎn Qiáo	Jiuyan Bridge	2
九寨沟	Jiǔzhài Gōu	Jiuzhai Valley Scenic and Historic Interest Area	5
K			
康定情歌	Kāngdìng Qínggē	Kangding Love Song, name of a song	1
宽窄巷子	Kuānzhǎi Xiàng·zi	the Wide and Narrow Alleys, ancient streets in Chengdu	2
L			
辣子鸡	Là·zi Jī	Peppery Chicken	7
赖汤圆	Lài tāngyuán	Lai Glutinous Rice Balls	7
乐山	Lèshān	Leshan City, a city in Sichuan Province	5
乐山大佛	Lèshān Dàfó	Leshan Giant Buddha	5
凉山	Liángshān	Liangshan Yi Autonomous Prefecture in Sichuan	10
梁平	Liángpíng	Liangping District, a district in Chongqing Municipality	6
刘备	Liú Bèi	Liu Bei (161-223, the first emperor of Kingdom of Shu from the Three Kingdoms era of China)	2
M			
麻婆豆腐	Mápó Dòu·fu	Stir-Fried Tofu in Hot Sauce	7
蒙顶甘露	Méngdǐng Gānlù	a green tea produced in Mengding Mountain	8

附录2：词汇总表
Appendix 2: Vocabulary

续表
Continued

绵阳	Miányáng	Mianyang City, a city in Sichuan Province	6
绵竹	Miánzhú	Mianzhu City, a county-level city in Sichuan Province	6
缅甸	Miǎndiàn	Myanmar	4
苗族	Miáozú	Miao People	10
岷江	Mínjiāng	Minjiang River	2
茉莉花	Mò·lì Huā	Jasmine Flower, name of a song	1
N			
南河	Nánhé	Nanhe River	2
Q			
羌族	Qiāngzú	Qiang People	10
青城山	Qīngchéng Shān	Mount Qingcheng	5
青城雪芽	Qīngchéng Xuěyá	a green tea produced in Qingcheng Mountain	8
青羊宫	Qīngyáng Gōng	the Qingyang Temple	4
R			
汝瓷	Rǔcí	Ru Porcelain	8
S			
四川省川剧院	Sìchuānshěng Chuānjùyuàn	Sichuan Opera Troupe	6
蜀	Shǔ	an ancient state name of Sichuan area in history; another name for Sichuan Province	2
蜀南竹海	Shǔnán Zhúhǎi	Southern Sichuan Bamboo Sea	5
双流国际机场	Shuāngliú Guójì Jīchǎng	Shuangliu International Airport	3
松潘	Sōngpān	Songpan County, a county under the jurisdiction of Aba Tibetan and Qiang Autonomous Prefecture in Sichuan Province	5
T			
太平园站	Tàipíngyuán Zhàn	Taipingyuan Station	3

续表
Continued

糖醋里脊	Tángcù Lǐjǐ	Sweet and Sour Fillet	7
糖醋排骨	Tángcù Páigǔ	Sweet and Sour Spare Ribs	7
淘宝	Táobǎo	Taobao, an online shopping mall	9
天安门广场	Tiān'ānmén Guǎngchǎng	Tian'anmen Square	10
天府国际机场	Tiānfǔ Guójì Jīchǎng	Tianfu International Airport	3
天府通	Tiānfǔtōng	Tianfutong Card	3
天府通应用程序	Tiānfǔtōng Yīngyòng Chéngxù	Tianfutong application	3
W			
微信	Wēixìn	WeChat	9
文化宫站	Wénhuàgōng Zhàn	Cultural Palace Station	3
文殊院	Wénshū Yuàn	the Wenshu Monastery	4
武侯祠	Wǔhóu Cí	the Wuhou Shrine, Marquis Wu's Shrine	4
武侯区	Wǔhóu Qū	Wuhou District, a district of Chengdu City	2
X			
西昌	Xīchāng	Xichang, a city in Sichuan Province	10
西湖	Xīhú	West Lake	1
洗面桥	Xǐmiàn Qiáo	Ximian Bridge	2
咸烧白	Xián Shāobái	Sichuan-style steamed pork with pickled mustard leaves	6
校友林	Xiàoyǒu Lín	Alumni Grove	1
兴文石林	Xīngwén Shílín	Xingwen Stone Forest	5
Y			
彝族	Yízú	Yi People	10
银杏大道	Yínxìng Dàdào	Ginkgo Avenue	1

附录2：词汇总表
Appendix 2：Vocabulary

续表
Continued

银杏节	Yínxìng Jié	Ginkgo Festival	1
Z			
浙江	Zhèjiāng	Zhejiang Province	10
支付宝	Zhīfùbǎo	Alipay	9
钟水饺	Zhōng Shuǐjiǎo	Zhong Dumpling	7
诸葛亮	Zhūgě Liàng	Zhuge Liang (181-234), premier of the Shu state	4
自贡	Zìgòng	Zigong City, a city in Sichuan Province	6
自贡恐龙博物馆	Zìgòng Kǒnglóng Bówùguǎn	Zigong Dinosaur Museum	5

附录3：音频、视频文本
Appendix 3: Audio and Video Scripts

第一单元　乐学成都

任务一

欢迎大家来到我们学校。我们从南门进入校园，首先看到的是高大的主楼，主楼广场上摆放着鲜花，旗杆上挂着中国的国旗——五星红旗。穿过主楼右边的通道，我们进入漂亮的银杏大道。大道的东边是东湖，左边是校友林。校友林的后边还有一个湖，叫西湖。湖里有优雅的天鹅和可爱的鸭子。湖边是同学们运动、晨读和休闲的好去处。沿着银杏大道一直往前走，我们会经过学校的教学楼。图书馆和时间广场在教学楼的对面，从早到晚，陪伴着每一个学子，努力追求梦想。再往前走，就是食堂。这里环境舒适，菜品丰富。食堂的后边是一座座整齐的宿舍楼，那里是同学们在大学里温暖的家。校园的东边有各种运动场所：篮球场、足球场、网球场、游泳馆和体育中心。体育中心可以举办运动会和各种大型活动。如果从学校西门进入校园，你会看到一条美丽的小河，河边是湿地公园。校医院也在西门的旁边。

这里，春天桃红李白，夏天绿树成荫，秋天银杏金黄，冬天梅花飘香。这里，将开启你美好的大学时光。

任务二

情景：杜无羡和以前的中文老师打电话聊天，聊在中国的学习和生活。

文老师：你好，我是文老师。请问你是哪位？

杜无羡：文老师，您好！我是杜无羡。半年没联系了，您好吗？

文老师：杜无羡，是你啊！我挺好的。很高兴接到你的电话。你在中国习惯了吗？

杜无羡：差不多习惯了，只是从星期一到星期五都有课，比较忙。

文老师：早上几点上课？

杜无羡：八点半开始上课。天气冷的时候，起床特别困难。

文老师：下午也有课吗？

杜无羡：除了星期五下午没课，别的下午都有课。不过，下午一般只有两节课，从两点半上到四点多。

文老师：下课后你一般做什么？

杜无羡：我常常去健身，或者约朋友打打篮球、踢踢足球。

文老师：那很充实嘛。你的汉语现在学得怎么样了？

杜无羡：比刚来中国的时候好多了，现在差不多可以和中国朋友用汉语聊天了。

文老师：你们的汉语课多吗？

杜无羡：不多，这学期一周只有六节课，别的都是专业课。不过，听说下学期有一些和中国文化有关的选修课，我很感兴趣。

文老师：那挺好的！我看了你的朋友圈，里面有很多有意思的照片，看来你去了不少地方啊。

杜无羡：是啊，我非常喜欢旅游。有时候，学校也会组织一些旅游活动。

文老师：这样很好，对你学习汉语很有帮助。

任务三

情景：丹枫和杜无羡在逛校园。

丹　枫：我们学校真漂亮，有这么多花，这么多树！

杜无羡：是啊，早晨在湖边散散步，看看天鹅，听听鸟叫，挺舒服的。

丹　枫：真幸福！

杜无羡：你知道吗？现在是我们学校最漂亮的季节。每年十一月，校园里的银杏叶都黄了，金灿灿的，很多人来学校照相。学校每年还举办银杏节呢。

丹　枫：银杏节是什么？

杜无羡：银杏节就是我们学校为了"赏银杏美景，品传统文化"而举办的活动。这时候，校园里有各种各样的活动，比如，猜谜语、音乐会、健身运动什么的，还有摄影展和美食展。

丹　枫：那一定很热闹吧！

杜无羡：当然！你看，那儿有人正在拍照呢！

丹　枫：看见了。那个女孩还穿着裙子呢！太冷了吧。

杜无羡：你们女孩都喜欢"美丽冻人"。

丹　枫：哈哈哈！不过今天天气确实好，阳光灿烂，树叶金黄，确实美！来，给我也照一张吧。

杜无羡：好。笑一笑！

（拍照以后）

丹　枫：谢谢！

杜无羡：累了吧？去喝杯咖啡休息一下？

丹　枫：好啊，去哪儿？

杜无羡：一楼有个咖啡馆，去那里怎么样？

丹　枫：好主意，听说那儿环境特别棒！走！

任务四

情景：在生日聚会上，丹枫、杜无羡和何蓉蓉一起聊天。

杜无羡：丹枫，生日快乐！

丹　枫：谢谢你，杜无羡！

杜无羡：这是送给你的生日礼物，你看看喜欢不喜欢？

丹　枫：音乐光盘！全是中国音乐，太好了！我很喜欢。谢谢！

杜无羡：上面有《康定情歌》和《成都》这两首歌。

丹　枫：哇，是我来这儿听得最多的两首歌，百听不厌。

杜无羡：看来我买对了。

丹　枫：谢谢！喝点儿什么？果汁还是茉莉花茶？

杜无羡：果汁吧，谢谢！

丹　枫：对不起，我忘了介绍了。何蓉蓉，这是我的同学杜无羡。杜无羡，这是我朋友何蓉蓉，她在读研究生，我们常常一起散步。

何蓉蓉：你好，杜无羡！认识你很高兴。

杜无羡：认识你我也很高兴。读研怎么样？

何蓉蓉：挺忙的。虽然课不多，但是经常要去图书馆看书查资料，还要去实验室工作，跟导师见面，不过这样能学到很多东西。

杜无羡：那你每天有时间锻炼身体或者放松一下吗？

何蓉蓉：不是每天都有时间。不过，我每周都会找时间放松一下，约朋友去校内的美食街吃吃饭，或者去咖啡馆聊聊天。

杜无羡：我也很少出校园，大部分时间都在学校里。校园里的生活很便利，银行、书店、咖啡馆、小餐馆、小超市……什么都有。

何蓉蓉：是啊，平时学习忙，我们都不爱出校门。不过，一到周末，我就喜欢去学校附近的购物中心。那里是逛街、吃饭、休闲娱乐的好地方。周末就更热闹了。

杜无羡：是吗？那我有空也去逛逛。

第二单元 探 源 天 府

任务一

成都在中国西南，位于四川盆地西部、成都平原中部。它是四川省省会，也是西南地区的中心城市之一。现在，成都有锦江区、成华区、武侯区、高新区等14个区。其中锦江区商业发达，有名的太古里、春熙路就在这个区。目前成都常住人口已经超过1600万了。

成都平原地势平坦，有很多大大小小的河流，岷江是很重要的一条。它有两条支流经过成都，一条叫府河，另外一条叫南河。府河和南河也叫作"锦江"，是成都的"母亲河"。西北部有"都江堰水利工程"，所以成都平原农业发达，物产丰富，有"天府之国"的美称。很早以前，成都人就开始养蚕、织锦，这里的丝锦非常漂亮，也很有名，所以成都也叫"锦官城"或者"锦城"。

成都也是一座国家历史文化名城，是古蜀文化开始的重要地方。3000多年前人们就开始在这里居住生活了，而成都这个名字也已经用了2000多年了。悠久的历史在成都留下了很多故事和名胜古迹。比如，成都市的金沙遗址，就是大概3000年前古蜀时期人们的活动场所。1700多年前的三国时期，成都是蜀国都城，这段历史上出现了刘备、诸葛亮、关羽和张飞等这些著名政治军事人物。成都还是世界上最早使用纸币的地方，那时候的纸币叫作"交子"。除了这些以外，成都还有很多的街道名称都跟成都的历史和人们的生活有关，比如，"琴台路""宽窄巷子""洗面桥"等。

天气好的时候，如果你有时间，约个朋友逛逛成都那些有故事的大街小巷，一定很有意思。

任务二

情景： 新学期快开始了，丹枫和赵丽川在教学楼门口遇见了。

赵丽川：丹枫你好！

丹　枫：学姐好！成都真大啊！昨天从机场到学校，我们坐出租车坐了差不多一个小时。

赵丽川：是有点儿远。机场在成都南边，我们学校在成都西北边。

丹　枫：坐出租车来学校的时候，我看到路上有很多车、很多人。他们看起来都很忙。可是为什么我听说成都很休闲呢？

赵丽川：以前成都城区不大，人们生活比较休闲。可是现在城区越来越大，人口也越来越多，房子比以前贵多了，生活也就不轻松了。每天很多人要坐公交车、地铁或者开车上下班，所以人多车也多，大家都很忙。

丹　枫：这样啊。成都人口这么多，堵车吗？

赵丽川：是啊，一到上下班的时候就堵车。

丹　枫：我还看见路两边都有树和花，堵车的时候，看看花草树木，心情可能会好一点儿吧。

赵丽川：我也这么觉得。成都正在建设宜居城市，所以建了很多公园。街道两边和公园里种了各种树和花，一年四季花开不断，生机勃勃。

丹　枫：现在已经是秋天了吧，秋天成都有什么花呢？

赵丽川：每年八月到十月成都很多地方都能看到芙蓉花，有的是粉色的，有的是白色的。芙蓉花是成都的市花，所以成都也叫"蓉城"。你看到芙蓉花了吗？

丹　枫：我还不认识芙蓉花呢。

赵丽川：没关系，你先好好休息。如果你有时间，星期六我带你逛逛成都，去看看芙蓉花。

丹枫：好啊好啊。先谢谢你了！

任务三

情景： 留学生何蓉蓉、夏涛和中国学生赵丽川一起参观天府广场。

赵丽川：到了，这里就是天府广场。

夏　涛：真漂亮！我知道北京的天安门广场，上海的人民广场，这里为什么叫天府广场呢？

赵丽川：这跟四川的历史和地理有关。成都平原很早以前就有一个美丽的名字——"天府之国"。

夏　涛："天府之国"是什么意思？

赵丽川："天府"是"天然的府库，物产丰富"的意思，"国"这里是"地方"的意思。"天府之国"就是物产丰富的地方。

何蓉蓉：是这样啊。那这里为什么物产丰富呢？

赵丽川：这是因为有都江堰水利工程，成都平原不旱不涝，粮食充裕，又很少有战争，所以人们生活富足安定。

夏　涛：原来是这样！

何蓉蓉：（用手指着太阳神鸟雕塑）你们看，广场中间这个雕塑是什么意思？

赵丽川：这个雕塑叫"太阳神鸟"，它的图案是在成都发现的。这个图案里的十二道阳光象征十二个月，四只神鸟象征四个季节，表达了大概三千年前古人对时间的认识和对太阳的崇拜。

何蓉蓉：明白了。太阳很重要，世界上很多文化里都有太阳崇拜。

夏　涛：的确，三千年前人们就知道一年有四季、十二个月，真了不起。这个"太阳神鸟"图案是在这个广场地下发现的吗？

赵丽川：不是，是在成都金沙遗址发现的，就在成都市区，离这里大概6公里。

何蓉蓉：听起来很有趣，我想去看看。

夏　涛：我也很感兴趣，想多了解一点儿成都的历史文化。

赵丽川：我们旁边就是成都博物馆，正好可以进去了解一下。今天我们先去这个博物馆看看，改天再去金沙遗址，怎么样？

何蓉蓉：好的，先去这个近的。

夏　涛：好，我们现在就过去吧。

任务四

情景：中国学生王成和林一诺、丁思尧一起买完东西后从商店里出来。

丁思尧：现在在中国，坐公交车、买东西都可以用手机付钱，太方便了。

林一诺：是啊，我现在常常忘记带钱和银行卡，但是我不会忘记带手机。我担心毕业以后回国会不习惯。

王　成：我也很长时间不用现金了。不过，你们知道吗，成都是世界上最早使用纸币的地方。

林一诺：纸币？纸做的钱吗？

王　成：是的，最早的纸币叫"交子"，差不多1000年前成都人就开始用它来买东西、卖东西了。

丁思尧：等等！"饺子"不是吃的东西吗？

王　成：是"交子"不是"饺子"，声调不一样，"交子"是第一声。

林一诺：那时候，用纸做钱，不担心有假钱吗？

王　成：我听说"交子"是用特别的纸和特别的技术做的，所以没有人能做假钱。

丁思尧：什么样的纸？

王　成：我也不知道。要是我知道，我就是有钱人了。

林一诺：哈哈，你真幽默！

王　成：成都有一条街叫"交子大道"，就是为了纪念纸币发明。

丁思尧：哦，我明白了，"交子"不是"饺子"，"交子"可以买"饺子"。

王　成：对，你的汉语越来越好了。

林一诺：对了，我还听说过其他有意思的街名，比如，"九眼桥""合江亭""锦里"，还有"洗面桥"什么的。

王　成：是的，成都历史悠久、文化深厚。你们知道吗，"洗面桥"这个名字就和三国时期的"刘备""关羽"有关。

林一诺："刘备"和"关羽"就是三国时期蜀国的皇帝和将军吧。

王　成：对。据说，一次战争中，关羽失败后被杀了，刘备非常伤心，就为他修了一座庙，每年都会去庙里纪念他。纪念之前，刘备都要在庙前小河桥边整装洗面，后来那里就叫作"洗面桥"。

丁思尧：虽然我不是太明白你说的话，但是我听说过关羽，我也很喜欢他。

林一诺：成都的历史很长，故事也很多。

王　成：是啊，以后有空的时候我们常出来逛逛，多了解一些成都的故事。

第三单元　宜居锦城

任务一

成都是一座很宜居的城市，气候很好。春秋两季气温适中，不冷不热；夏季温度不高，一般不超过35度；冬季气温大多在零度以上，很少下雪。这里空气比较湿润，对皮肤很好。另外，成都常常晚上下雨，早上就停了，就像杜甫的诗——《春夜喜雨》——里写的那样："随风潜入夜，润物细无声。"

如果你想来成都游玩的话，春秋两季来最好。你可以乘飞机、火车或者长途大巴来，非常方便。双流国际机场是西南地区的主要枢纽机场，有飞往中国大多数城市的航班，也有飞往亚洲、非洲、欧洲、美洲和大洋洲的航班。机场离市区只有半小时左右车程。从机场去市区可以乘机场大巴、地铁，或者打车。从机场去成都附近的景区还可以乘"景区直通车"。

成都有三个客运火车站，分别在成都市区的东边、南边和北边。长途汽车站也在市区。市区公共交通很发达，地铁、公共汽车、二环高架快速公交车班次都比较多，又快又方便。你只需要买一张天府通公交卡，车票九折，两小时以内还可以免费转公交车呢，也可以用手机下载天府通应用程序，直接扫码乘车。

街上还有很多出租车和网约车，可以带你到任何你想去的地方。你也可以骑上共享单车，走走停停，逛逛成都的大街小巷。

任务二

情境：赵丽川和林一诺在学校门口的有轨电车站等车，去机场接新生丹枫。

林一诺：你怎么想到坐有轨电车呢？

赵丽川：上个月有轨电车就通车了，我还没有坐过呢，想试试。

林一诺：我也没坐过。你知道怎么买票吗？

赵丽川：我昨天上网查过了，无人售票，刷公交卡就可以了。你带公交卡了吗？

林一诺：糟糕，我没带公交卡。刚才要出门的时候，看见下雨了，我拿了雨伞就出来了，把公交卡忘了。

赵丽川：没事儿，也可以上车投币。我有两块钱零钱，给你吧。

林一诺：太好了，谢谢！

赵丽川：不客气。我们先坐到终点站成都西站，然后转地铁去机场。

林一诺：看，这儿有线路图。我看看要坐多少站，我数数，一、二、三……还挺远的。

赵丽川：我们在成都西站下车，再转地铁4号线，然后在文化宫站转7号线，最后在太平园站转10号线就到机场了。

林一诺：这么麻烦啊！转这么多次车。

赵丽川：是有点麻烦，不过，我们不赶时间，既可以体验一下有轨电车，又不用担心堵车。

林一诺：下一班车还有多久？

赵丽川：我们去看看电子显示屏吧。

林一诺：下一班车还有2分钟到。太先进了！电子显示屏上有时间，有车次，还是中英文的呢。

赵丽川：车快来了。我们准备上车吧。

任务三

情景：春熙路地铁站地面处，王成等丹枫和林一诺一起去杜甫草堂等景点玩。

王　成：丹枫、林一诺！我在这儿。

（丹枫和林一诺走过来）

丹　枫：这儿人太多了。下车的人多，上车的人也很多。

王　成：没错，这里是市中心，当然比别的地方热闹一些。

林一诺：我每次来春熙路，这里都是人山人海的。

丹　枫：这么多人，我们回去的时候会不会等很久才能上车啊？

王　成：不会，差不多每3分钟就有一班地铁，所以不用担心。丹枫，你第一次坐成都地铁，觉得怎么样？

丹　枫：好快啊！你看我这张地铁票，背面有图案，很有意思。

王　成：对，地铁票背面的图案是成都十大景点。对了，你们怎么突然要来市区逛？

丹　枫：我来成都快一个月了，还没怎么逛过呢。前几天就约了林一诺，但总是下雨，不方便出来玩。

林一诺：昨天晚上又下雨了，我们担心今天还是不方便出来。

丹　枫：还好，今天早晨晴了。

王　成：成都常常晚上下雨，早上雨就停了，尤其是在春天。

林一诺：对，晚上听着雨声睡觉，我很喜欢。

王　成：成都的夜雨非常有名，有一首唐诗《春夜喜雨》，写的就是成都春天的夜雨。

林一诺：我知道，老师教过。很美的一首诗，作者叫杜甫，他以前住的地方就离这儿不远。

王　　成：对。他住的地方叫"杜甫草堂"，今天我们去看看。

（三人在春熙路地铁站地面处）

丹　　枫：我们怎么去呢？

林一诺：我们要去坐景区直通车，就在春熙路上车。

王　　成：那我们走这边。你们怎么要坐景区直通车？

林一诺：丹枫说想去几个地方，公交车没有景区直通车方便，因为公交车转车太麻烦了，等车也要花很多时间。

王　　成：好，那我们就去坐景区直通车。

任务四

情境：赵丽川和林一诺在双流机场第二航站楼到达门口接丹枫。

赵丽川：丹枫的航班是到T2航站楼吗？如果她坐国际航班的话，应该到T1吧。

林一诺：没错，是T2。她坐国际航班先到昆明，然后从昆明坐国内航班飞过来。

赵丽川：她的航班号是什么？

林一诺：CA 4414。

（二十分钟以后）

赵丽川：你看电子显示屏，她的航班到了，还很准时。她要取行李，应该还有一会儿才出来。

林一诺：嗯。我们把牌子举起来，上面有她的名字，她一出来就能看到我们。

（丹枫走到赵丽川和李一诺面前）

丹　　枫：你们好！我是丹枫。

林一诺：你好，丹枫！我是林一诺，她是赵丽川。学院让我们来机场接你。

丹　　枫：你们好！谢谢你们来接我。

赵丽川：坐那么久的飞机，你一定很累吧。

丹　　枫：还好。这个机场好大啊！又大又漂亮！中国的机场都这么大、这么漂亮吗？

赵丽川：大部分城市的机场都比较大。双流机场还不是最大的，只有T1和T2两个航站楼。不过，成都还有一个新机场，叫天府机场。

林一诺：对，我也听说了，成都有两个机场。

丹　枫：两个机场啊？那成都的交通太发达了。

林一诺：现在我们怎么回学校？

赵丽川：机场离市区挺近的，但我们学校在四环以外，比较远。我们可以坐机场大巴先转到市里，再转公交车到学校。

林一诺：她的行李有点儿多，要不我们直接坐出租车回学校？

赵丽川：好，我们三个人打车比较好。

第四单元　蜀都访胜

任务一

成都不但繁华时尚，而且拥有独特的人文景观和区域特色。市内的青羊宫，是中国有名的道教宫观之一。据说青羊宫在2000多年前就有了，现在的建筑物大多数是300多年前修建的。这里的传统建筑、雕塑、绘画和音乐都特别有意思。这里有世界上最全的道教资料，研究道教的人一定会到这里来。

除了独特的道教文化，成都还有历史悠久的佛教文化。比如文殊院这座寺庙，已经有大约1400年的历史了。和青羊宫差不多，它现在的建筑也是300年前重建的。文殊院在禅宗中的地位非常重要，是喜欢禅、研究禅的人常来的地方。

成都在三国文化中地位独特。著名的武侯祠，是纪念诸葛亮和刘备的地方。他们是1700多年前三国时期蜀国的丞相和皇帝。诸葛亮在中国历史文化中影响很大，是忠诚和智慧的象征。人们都很喜欢他，尊重他。

成都还有全世界都喜欢的大熊猫，它们的家就在市区东北边的大熊猫基地。在那儿，它们爬树、睡觉、吃竹子，样子可爱极了。

任务二

情境：赵丽川、杜无羡和王成聊成都名胜古迹。

赵丽川：杜无羡，我知道你对中国文化感兴趣，你去过青羊宫吗？

杜无羡：没有。青羊宫是什么地方？我还是第一次从你这儿听到。

赵丽川：是一座著名的道教宫观。在那里你可以了解宗教文化，也可以体验中国的传统艺术。

杜无羡：是这样啊！听说道教是中国的传统宗教，认为简单、自然的生活是最好的。

王　成：你说得对。老子、庄子的思想对中国传统文化影响很大，比如，"道法自然""清静无为"，这些都是我们熟悉的。

赵丽川："庄周梦蝶"的故事也很有名。庄子在梦中见到了蝴蝶，醒来以后，他不知道是他梦见了蝴蝶，还是蝴蝶梦见了他。

杜无羡：听起来真有意思！有机会的话，我真想多了解一下道教文化。

王　成：青羊宫除了道教文化，还有中国的传统建筑，这些建筑也体现了道教的哲学思想。另外，那里还有雕塑、楹联、绘画、音乐这些传统文化艺术。

杜无羡：还有音乐？有乐队和歌手表演吗？

赵丽川：（笑一下）主要是道教音乐，不是流行音乐。一般是在重要的道教节日表演。

王　成：对了，武术、太极拳也跟道教有关。在青羊宫你很有可能碰到高人呢。

杜无羡：哇，真的吗？我们什么时候去一趟，我正想多学习一点中国传统文化。

赵丽川：我们这个周末一起去，怎么样？青羊宫离我们这里不太远，交通也方便。

杜无羡：好的。我在手机上查一下，看看怎么走。

赵丽川：不用查了，咱们坐地铁2号线，在青羊宫站下，出来就到了。这个星期六上午9:00在学校西门见面，然后一起出发，怎么样？

杜无羡：好。

王　成：就这么定了！

任务三

情景：赵丽川、丁思尧和王成一起去参观文殊院。

丁思尧（进入寺庙，环顾四周）：文殊院的环境真不错，跟我们上次去过的青羊宫差不多，一进来就感觉很清静。

赵丽川：是啊，这里面有很多花草树木，没有什么噪声，人也没有那么匆忙。

王　成：放慢脚步，放松心情，体验慢生活。很多人来文殊院，就是为了这个目的。

赵丽川（手指雕像）：当然还可以体验这里的佛教艺术文化。文殊院在禅宗中的地位非常重要。

丁思尧：禅宗？好像不少西方人现在也喜欢禅了。他们对冥想很感兴趣。

王　成：准确地说，应该叫"打坐"，或者"静坐"。你看，就像这尊菩萨雕像一样。

赵丽川：算了，别难为丁思尧了，这个问题有点难，和翻译有关。

丁思尧：不要紧，虽然我弄不懂，但是至少可以看看这里的建筑、雕塑、书法什么的。

赵丽川（手指建筑）：文殊院现在的建筑是大约300年前重修的，是典型的清代四川西部风格。

赵丽川（手指雕塑）：里面的雕塑也大多是300年前的。

王　成（手指楹联）：楹联的书法也很漂亮，很多都是名人写的。

王　成（手指展览室）：文殊院还有展览室，用来展览中国书法和绘画作品。

丁思尧：我的书法作品也能在这里展览吗？我可是已经练了两年了！

任务四

情境：王成、赵丽川和杜无羡谈论武侯祠和熊猫基地。

王　成：杜无羡，成都的名胜古迹你差不多都去过了吧？

杜无羡：没有，还有很多地方没去过呢。听说武侯祠也不错，我想去参观一下。

赵丽川：武侯祠是纪念诸葛亮和刘备的地方。

杜无羡：他们是谁？

赵丽川：诸葛亮是1700年前三国时期蜀国的丞相，他是忠诚和智慧的象征。

杜无羡：那刘备也是三国时期的人吗？跟诸葛亮是什么关系？

王　成：刘备是三国时期蜀国的皇帝。诸葛亮是他的好助手。这两个人在中国历史和文化中影响很大。人们都很尊重他们。

赵丽川：事实上，诸葛亮在中国民间文化中影响更大。因为他不仅是忠诚和智慧的象征，而且还有仁爱、勤奋的美德。武侯祠的"武侯"指的就是诸葛亮。

王　成：对，三国时期的历史故事不仅在中国流行，在日本、越南等国家也有很多人知道。

杜无羡：那我更应该去看看了！除了武侯祠这样的名胜古迹，还有什么地方应该去参观一下？

赵丽川：可以去成都熊猫基地参观参观，大熊猫是全世界都喜欢的宝贝。熊猫基地就在成都的东北边，离咱们学校也不远。

王　成：在那里，你可以看见大大小小的熊猫，在一起爬树、睡觉、吃竹子，样子可爱极了。

杜无羡：非常感谢你们的介绍！我想以后去这些地方好好体验一下。

第五单元　绚美四川

任务一

每个假期都有很多人从四面八方来到成都。他们一般先在成都市区游玩，然后从这里出发，开始他们的四川之旅。从成都出发可以去很多特别有意思的地方，有的风景优美，有的历史悠久。比如，成都附近有千年水利工程"都江堰"、道教名山"青城山"。大多数第一次来成都的游客都会选择去这两个地方。稍远一点儿的乐山、峨眉山也非常受欢迎。乐山有著名的"乐山大佛"，峨眉山更是全国闻名的"佛教名山"。如果你想去再远一些的地方，可以选择九寨沟和黄龙。这两个地方很有名，风景很有特色，非常迷人。如果你有三四天的时间，就可以去川南地区。自贡恐龙博物馆、蜀南竹海、兴文石林都是你不能错过的好地方。如果你喜欢雪山、草原、峡谷、冰川这些自然风光，那就一定要去川西旅行了。

四川是一片神奇的土地，它会让来到这里的人流连忘返。你们要是来了成都，一定要找时间去四川各地旅行，看看山山水水，听听故事传说。旅行会让你更了解这个地方，也会让你更喜欢这个地方！

任务二

情境：王成、杜无羡和赵丽川聊五一旅游计划。

王　成：五一假期就快到了。我们出去玩儿几天吧！

杜无羡：我也想去旅游。我们去什么地方呢？

赵丽川：五一假期不长，我们就在成都附近玩儿吧！

王　成：杜无羡，你去过乐山和峨眉山吗？

杜无羡：没去过。这两个地方有什么特别的吗？

王　成：乐山最有名的是"乐山大佛"。

杜无羡："大佛"！一定很大吧？有多大呢？

赵丽川：据说"乐山大佛"有差不多二十层楼那么高！它的脚上可以坐100多个人呢！

杜无羡：这么大呀！简直就是一座山啊！

王　成：你说得对！"乐山大佛"依山而造，有"山是一尊佛，佛是一座山"的说法。你想象一下，1300多年以前，人们把一座山雕刻成一尊佛，是多么了不起的事情啊！

杜无羡：哇，我一定要去看看像山一样高大的"乐山大佛"。

王　成：我们还可以去峨眉山。峨眉山有"峨眉天下秀"的美名。那里的风景很漂亮。

赵丽川：峨眉山还是中国的佛教名山，山上有很多著名的寺庙。杜无羡，你可以去拜拜佛。

王　成：如果我们爬到"金顶"，能看到云海和佛光就太幸运了！

杜无羡：我想"云海"是像海一样的云吧。那"金顶"是什么？"佛光"又是什么呢？

王　成："金顶"是峨眉山的山顶。"佛光"嘛，据说是一个神奇的光环。运气好的话，你可以看到自己的影子在里面，你走动，光环也会跟你一起动。

杜无羡：哇，太神奇了！希望我们运气好。对了，在峨眉山能看见大熊猫吗？

赵丽川：大熊猫可能看不到，但一定能见到很多猴子。峨眉山的猴子很有趣，不过我们还是要小心。

杜无羡：为什么？

王　成：到时候你就知道了！

赵丽川：杜无羡，别忘了准备点儿零食！

任务三

情景：杜无羡、王成和赵丽川在清水河边聊暑假去哪儿旅游。

杜无羡：上次我们去了乐山和峨眉山，很好玩！暑假我们去哪儿呢？

王　成：暑假我们去远一点儿的地方吧。

赵丽川：好啊，我想去九寨沟，以前去过一次，太美了，想再去一次。

杜无羡：我听说过九寨沟，好像那里的水很漂亮。

赵丽川：没错！"九寨归来不看水"就是说看过了九寨沟的水，别的地方的水就不用再看了！九寨沟有壮观的瀑布，还有五颜六色的"海子"，就像一个童话世界。

杜无羡："海子"是什么？

赵丽川："海子"就是湖，是当地人的叫法。

杜无羡：我都等不及了，想马上去那儿！

王　成：去九寨沟就一定要去黄龙，两个地方离得也不远。

杜无羡：什么"龙"？

王　成：黄龙。从远处看，那儿像一条黄色的巨龙。

杜无羡：那我们一定要去看看。

王　成：但是，那里的海拔更高一些，有些人在黄龙会出现高原反应。你们会不会有高原反应？

赵丽川：我不会！我去过海拔4000多米的地方，都没有高原反应。

杜无羡：我身体这么好，也不会！去黄龙要爬山吗？

王　成：对，我们要到山上去看"人间瑶池"！

杜无羡：什么"池"？是"水池"的"池"吗？

王　成：是"瑶池"，中国的神话故事里神仙住的地方，当然很美！黄龙被叫作"人间瑶池"，可以想象，那儿的景色一定漂亮极了。

杜无羡：也是去看水吗？

王　成：对。黄龙的水五彩斑斓。

杜无羡：九寨沟的水很美，黄龙的水也很美。到底哪个更美呢？

赵丽川：你去看了就知道了！

杜无羡：这两个地方在哪儿？离成都多远？

王　成：在阿坝州，离成都两三百公里吧。

赵丽川：这两个地方都是"世界自然遗产"和"国家5A级旅游景区"！到了四川不去九寨沟和黄龙就像到了北京不去故宫、长城一样遗憾！

任务四

情境：杜无羡、王成和赵丽川讨论暑假旅游的方式。

杜无羡：我们暑假去九寨沟和黄龙旅游。怎么去呢？

赵丽川：成都有到九寨沟的航班，我们可以坐飞机去。

王　成：机票多贵啊！再说，这么近，不用坐飞机吧！

杜无羡：有高铁吗？高铁又快又便宜。上次我们坐高铁去峨眉山，多舒服啊！

王　成：去九寨沟没有高铁，但是有大巴。

赵丽川：对啊，客运站肯定有去九寨沟的班车。我们可以在网上查查票价和时间。

王　成：也可以参加旅游团，导游帮我们安排好吃、住、行，我们只管玩儿，多方便啊！

赵丽川：参加旅游团不好玩！我上次就是跟团去的。基本上就是"上车睡觉，下车拍照"，没什么意思！

杜无羡：你们俩都有驾照，我们可以自己开车去，怎么样？

王　成：你是说自驾游啊！这个主意不错！我喜欢开车，一次开四五个小时都没问题！

赵丽川：太好了！那我们就租一辆车，沿着九环线慢慢玩儿。

杜无羡："九环线"是什么？

王　成：喔，"九环线"是一条环形的旅游路线，从成都出发经过松潘到九寨沟，再经过江油最后回到成都，一路可以欣赏各种风光，是很受欢迎的自驾线。一会儿我在地图上找给你看看。

杜无羡：好极了！那我们就自驾游吧！

赵丽川：我同意！我们现在就开始准备吧。出发前要在网上预订好住的地方，还要提前买好自驾游的保险！

王　成：对，安全第一！

赵丽川：杜无羡，你一定要准备好相机喔！你肯定会在路上不停地拍照的！

第六单元　蜀风艺海

任务一

四川地区历史悠久、文化灿烂、民俗丰富，今天我们就来看看这里有哪些具有地方特色的节庆习俗和传统工艺。

春节是中国最重要的节日。四川人在春节前要"打扬尘"，也就是开展一年内最大的室内清洁。小孩子要给长辈磕头拜年，长辈会给小孩子发"压岁钱"。春节那几天，大家去亲戚家"走人户"，也就是穿着新衣服，带着茶叶、点心、酒等礼品到亲戚家里拜年。

每年清明节，都江堰市会举办"清明放水节"。这个传统文化活动已经有1000多年的历史了，一方面是为了纪念李冰父子，他们二人在2200多年前带领大家修建都江堰水利工程，造福成都平原；另一方面也象征着一年春耕的开始，人们祈求五谷丰登、国泰民安。

除此以外，广元市还有一个"女儿节"，在每年的9月1日，这是纪念中国唯一的女皇帝武则天的。这一天，女子们会穿上新衣服，到河边游玩。

四川的传统工艺也十分发达，有多项非物质文化遗产。成都在西汉时代就是漆器生产的中心城市。历史资料证明，养蚕的始祖生长在今天四川的绵阳地区，"蜀锦"是中国"四大名锦"之一，"蜀绣"也特别有名，历史悠久。在晋代，蜀锦、蜀绣就成了"蜀中之宝"。"自贡剪纸"有3000多年的历史，风格独特、图案丰富、中外闻名。另外，四川民间的绘画丰富多彩，绵竹、夹江和梁平这三个县就有驰名中外的木版年画，其中的"绵竹年画"色彩丰富、风格独特，是中国"四大年画"之一。

好了，说了这么多四川地区特有的节日、活动和艺术作品，大家一定要去各个博物馆好好欣赏，去四川的各个城市好好玩玩！

任务二

情景：王成和杜无羡，何蓉蓉谈京剧和川剧。

王　成：何蓉蓉、杜无羡，好久不见！

杜无羡、何蓉蓉：你好，王成，好久不见！

王　成：你们看过川剧吗？

何蓉蓉：没有，但我在北京看过京剧。

杜无羡：京剧？川剧？是什么呀？我都没看过。

何蓉蓉：我虽然看过京剧，但是也说不清楚。王成，你给我们讲讲吧。

王　成：好啊。京剧是中国影响最大的一种戏曲，全国很多地方都能看到，尤其在北京最受欢迎。川剧主要在四川、重庆等西南地区流行。两种剧的唱腔是不一样的，伴奏用的乐器也不同。

杜无羡：什么是唱腔？

王　成：唱腔就是戏剧的唱法。川剧是用四川方言唱的，学习了各地的唱法，其中最有特点的是高腔。

杜无羡：我明白了，在四川应该听听川剧。

王　成：川剧还有一个特别有意思的表演——变脸！

何蓉蓉：变脸是什么啊？

王　成：变脸，就是川剧演员在表演的时候突然改变脸上的面具，就像换了一个角色一样！而且他们的动作非常快，观众根本看不出他们是怎么变的。

何蓉蓉：我看京剧的时候，觉得京剧的脸谱很有意思，没看过川剧的变脸，想去看看他们有什么不一样。

王　成：你真的应该去看看，川剧除了变脸以外，还有"喷火"表演呢。演员可以从嘴里吐出火来。

杜无羡：太神奇了，去哪里能看到呢？

王　成：在成都锦里、宽窄巷子的一些茶馆和饭店有时候会有川剧表演。如果你们想看正式的表演，最好去四川省川剧院。

任务三

王成介绍坝坝宴。

进门之后，您看到的就是"坝坝宴"，这是四川地区传统特色宴席。在成都平原，有红白喜事的时候，人们会请左邻右舍、亲朋好友来大吃一顿。由于宴席是摆在自家的院坝里，所以叫作"坝坝宴"，又叫"九斗碗"。为什么又叫"九斗碗"呢？"九斗碗"也叫"九大碗"。在中国文化里，数字"九"表示数量多，而"斗碗"在四川方言里就是"大碗"的意思。所以"九斗碗"的意思就是摆了很多道菜的宴席。这些菜大多是蒸菜，有蒸鱼、蒸鸡、蒸鸭、蒸排骨、咸烧白等，菜品丰富，场面热闹。

坝坝宴也非常讲究。首先，虽然食材常见，但是要做得很好吃；其次，一定要有鱼，意思是"有余"，生活富足；还有，分量也要大，要用大碗装，不用盘子装；最后，摆多少碗也是有讲究的。有钱人家摆十　碗，而穷人家只摆七碗，但是不能摆十碗，因为"十"的发音也可以是"石头"的"石"，而"石碗"是给动物用的。

任务四

情景：赵丽川带杜无羡去一家小店买拖鞋。

店　主：（四川话）随便看，随便看，想买点儿啥子？

赵丽川：（四川话）他想买双拖鞋儿，相因点儿的。

店　主：（四川话）我这儿"háizi"多得很，随便选。

杜无羡：我不要"孩子"，不要"孩子"。我买"鞋子"。

店　主：（四川话）我才不敢卖娃儿。

赵丽川：你别着急。刚才我和老板说的是四川话，老板说的"háizi"就是鞋子的意思。我说的"相因的拖鞋儿"就是"便宜的拖鞋"。

杜无羡：哦，我晓得了，四川话里"háizi"就是鞋子，相因就是便宜的意思。

店　主：（四川话）你可以嘛，都会说四川话了。

赵丽川：（四川话）老板儿，这双"háizi"多少钱？

店　主：（四川话）十块。

杜无羡：四块，这么"相因"啊。

店　主：（四川话）你先试一下这双孩儿

（赵丽川让杜无羡试鞋）

赵丽川：你试试这双鞋吧。

店　主：（四川话）你看嘛，巴适得很。

杜无羡："巴适得很"，老板说的是什么意思啊？

赵丽川："巴适"就是"很好"的意思。你觉得这双鞋怎么样？

杜无羡：巴适得很。就要这双吧。

赵丽川：（四川话）老板儿，他就要这双了。

店　主：（四川话）要得。

第七单元　百味物语

任务一

"老板儿，来一个回锅肉！"这是我们常常在四川的饭馆里听到的。回锅肉作为川菜的一个代表，不仅四川人爱吃，其他地方的人也喜欢吃。作为中国八大菜系之一的川菜，味道独特，全国闻名，所以有"食在中国，味在四川"的说法。

相遇天府
——中文视听说
Encountering Sichuan: Chinese Video-watching, Listening and Speaking

　　川菜的特点是：食材广泛，做法多样，百菜百味。食材除了常见的各种肉类和蔬菜以外，还有不少山珍河鲜。川菜的基本味道有五种：麻、辣、咸、甜、酸。它们又可以组合成不同的味道，比如，又麻又辣的麻婆豆腐，甜中有辣的宫保鸡丁，酸酸甜甜的糖醋排骨和混合了麻、辣、咸、甜、酸五种味道的怪味鸡。川菜的烹饪方法至少有几十种，比如，炒、烧、炖、蒸、煮等。四川还有很多小吃，比如，辣得让人"流泪"的伤心凉粉、"煮时不浑汤，吃时三不沾"的赖汤圆和制作时会发出"砰、砰、砰"三声响的"三大炮"。火锅、串串、冒菜也都是非常有名的四川美食！其中，火锅已经成了四川的名片，所以有人说："到了四川如果不吃火锅，就等于没有到过四川。"

　　听了这些介绍，你是不是也想去尝一尝四川美食呢？

任务二

情景：杜无羡去王成家，看到赵丽川和王成正在做火锅。

杜无羡：厨房里这么多东西，你们在做什么？

赵丽川：我们一会儿吃火锅，需要准备很多东西。你看，这些是蔬菜和肉，那些是调料，这是锅底。

杜无羡：哇！锅底里有好多辣椒啊！太可怕了！

赵丽川：我是四川人，喜欢吃辣椒。

王　成：大多数四川人很喜欢吃辣的东西。

杜无羡：为什么呢？

王　成：主要是和气候有关系。四川经常下雨，空气潮湿，人们容易生病，冬天阴冷，所以吃饭时菜里加点儿辣椒，吃的时候会全身出汗，湿气和寒气会跟着汗水一起排出来，就不容易生病了。

杜无羡：原来是这样啊。看来吃辣椒对身体好啊。

赵丽川：火锅准备好了，大家都过来坐下，一起吃吧。

杜无羡：谢谢！来成都两年多了，我还是第一次吃火锅。该怎么吃呢？

王　成：很简单，一是煮，把肉、土豆什么的先放进去煮，这些菜需要比较长的时间才能熟；二是烫，肥牛、毛肚、鸭肠很快就能熟，烫一烫就可以吃了。

赵丽川：我们一般先吃肉再吃菜。你烫一片肥牛试试，你从一数到十五就可以吃了。

杜无羡：听起来很有意思啊！好，我试试。（杜无羡试了后）真的很辣！

附录3：音频、视频文本
Appendix 3：Audio and Video Scripts

任务三

情景：赵丽川、丹枫和华锦在饭馆外面讨论四川菜。

赵丽川：看，这儿有家川菜馆，我们吃川菜怎么样？

丹　枫：天啊！我不想再吃川菜了，太辣了。昨天朋友请我吃了辣子鸡，辣得我眼泪都流出来了！

华　锦：我也是，昨天我吃了麻婆豆腐，好麻啊！

赵丽川：实际上，川菜有很多种味道，可以说"百菜百味"！除了麻辣味，还有五香味、鱼香味、甜辣味等。不吃麻、辣的，可以尝尝这些味道啊！

丹　枫：是吗？那你给我们介绍几个菜吧！

赵丽川：没问题，我们进去坐下来慢慢说吧。

丹　枫：好的。走，华锦，我们进去。

（进入川菜馆坐下来，赵丽川指着菜单上的图片介绍）

赵丽川：你们看。这个宫保鸡丁味道是甜辣的，很多留学生都喜欢；这是糖醋里脊，酸酸甜甜的，吃起来棒极了；还有这个鱼香肉丝是鱼香味的，也很受欢迎。

华　锦：宫保鸡丁听起来挺好的，因为我喜欢吃鸡肉。诶，什么是甜辣味？

赵丽川：甜辣味就是甜甜的，稍微有点儿辣。

丹　枫：我喜欢酸甜味的，所以糖醋里脊好像不错！但是我不喜欢鱼香肉丝，因为我不爱吃鱼，刺太多了，太麻烦！

华　锦：我也不喜欢吃鱼，我受不了鱼腥味儿。

赵丽川：哈哈，别担心，鱼香肉丝里是没有鱼的。

丹　枫：真奇怪，没有鱼，怎么叫鱼香肉丝呢？

赵丽川：鱼香是一种味道！

华　锦：什么样的味道？像什么呢？

赵丽川：我也说不清楚，你们尝一尝就知道了！

丹　枫：那我们就尝尝这三道菜吧！

任务四

情景：赵丽川给丹枫和杜无羡介绍四川的小吃。

丹　枫：我们听说四川的小吃又多又好吃，你能给我们介绍一下吗？

赵丽川：好啊！最受欢迎的有伤心凉粉、蛋烘糕、串串、钵钵鸡什么的。

杜无羡：伤心凉粉？凉粉怎么会伤心？

173

赵丽川：伤心凉粉是四川的一种小吃，和移民到四川的客家人有关。客家人的故乡在广东，他们思念家乡时会做凉粉，因为思念而伤心，所以叫伤心凉粉。还有一种说法是：伤心凉粉特别辣，吃的时候会辣出眼泪，别人还以为遇到了什么伤心事。

丹　枫：好有意思，那你最喜欢的小吃是什么？

赵丽川：我最喜欢夫妻肺片，口感很棒！

杜无羡：夫妻肺片是一对夫妻做的吗？

赵丽川：对，据说是一位姓郭的成都人和他的妻子一起发明的。主要用的是牛肉和牛杂，不过没有牛肺喔。

丹　枫：名字叫夫妻肺片，为什么没有牛肺？

赵丽川：因为他们发现牛肺的口感不好，所以没用牛肺。

杜无羡：除了这些，有面食类的小吃吗？我喜欢吃面食。

赵丽川：当然有，比如，担担面，以前是用扁担挑在肩上去卖，所以叫担担面。

丹　枫：太有意思了，还有其他的面食类小吃吗？

赵丽川：还有钟水饺。

杜无羡：是不是就是中国北方的水饺？

赵丽川：不一样，中国北方的水饺馅儿里面一般都有蔬菜，但是钟水饺是纯肉馅儿的。

丹　枫：我喜欢吃肉。杜无羡，今天晚上我们就去吃钟水饺，怎么样？

杜无羡：好的。

第八单元　蓉城茶香

任务一

中国是茶树的原产地、茶叶的故乡，是世界上饮茶、制茶最早的国家。几千年前，就在中国的云南、贵州和四川等地发现了野生茶树。四川作为茶的原产地之一，茶文化历史悠久。这里被认为是中国甚至世界种植、制作、饮用茶叶的起源地之一。四川有很多大山，有良好的气候和地理环境，所以四川的茶也特别好喝。全国闻名的茶就有好几种，其中比较有名的有：峨眉毛峰、蒙顶甘露、青城雪芽、峨眉竹叶青等。

俗话说，"天下茶馆数中国，中国茶馆数四川"。四川人尤其爱喝茶，爱泡茶馆。在四川，到处都有茶馆。坐在茶馆里，叫上一杯盖碗茶，茶客们可以看川剧、打盹儿，也可以看看闲书，或者三三两两在一块摆摆龙门阵。有时候，旁边还有掏耳朵的、擦皮鞋的、算命看相的，大家都很开心自在。

四川独特的喝茶方式以及有特色的茶具，引起了许多国内外游客的兴趣。他们来到四川体验川茶文化。川茶体现了四川文化迷人的魅力，体现了四川人悠闲的生活。

任务二

情景：杜无羡、丹枫和中国朋友赵丽川聊成都的特色茶馆。

杜无羡：今天天气真好！

丹　枫：是啊！听说成都的茶馆很有名。来这么久了，我还没去过茶馆呢。我们去喝茶怎么样？

杜无羡：好主意！赵丽川，我们去哪儿喝？

赵丽川：那要看你们想去什么地方，想喝什么茶了。

杜无羡：哦，那你给我们介绍介绍吧。

赵丽川：我们四川人有句话，"头上晴天少，眼前茶馆多"，意思是我们这儿晴天不多，茶馆特别多。今天的天气这么好，最适合去喝坝坝茶了。

丹　枫：坝坝茶是什么茶？

赵丽川：（出声笑一下）坝坝茶不是一种茶。在四川方言里，露天的场地就叫坝坝。坝坝茶就是在露天的场地晒着太阳喝茶。竹椅、矮桌、一碗盖碗茶、暖暖的阳光，几个朋友摆着龙门阵，想想都觉得美！

杜无羡：等等，等等。盖碗茶是什么？摆龙门阵又是什么？

赵丽川：盖碗茶呀，是四川人喝茶的一种方式，很有特色，从茶具到服务都有讲究。你们去喝了就明白了。摆龙门阵呢，也是四川方言，简单地说就是聊天。四川人喜欢坐下来跟朋友慢慢地聊天，这就叫摆龙门阵。

杜无羡：明白了。我们去哪儿喝坝坝茶呢？

赵丽川：成都最有名的坝坝茶馆要数人民公园的鹤鸣茶馆，生意特别好，天气好的时候，去晚了还没座位呢。文殊院、百花潭公园、府南河边都有露天茶座，也很不错。

丹　枫：贵不贵？太贵了我可不去！

赵丽川：（出声笑一下）平民消费！人均不到二十块钱，叫上一碗茶可以坐上大半天。

杜无羡：说得我都等不及了。走，我们马上出发！

任务三

情景：丹枫和杜无羡去茶馆喝茶，听茶博士静妹儿介绍四川茶和盖碗茶。

静妹儿：请坐！请问你们喝什么茶？这是茶单。

丹　枫：能给我们介绍一下吗？蒙顶甘露、峨眉竹叶青、碧潭飘雪，有什么不同？

静妹儿：好的！四川主要产绿茶、红茶和花茶。峨眉山和蒙顶山是两大著名产地，茶单上这些茶都是这两个地方产的。蒙顶甘露和峨眉竹叶青是绿茶，而碧潭飘雪是花茶。

杜无羡：如果我们喝盖碗茶，应该选什么茶呢？

静妹儿：喝盖碗茶呢，最好选碧潭飘雪，而竹叶青像竹叶，用玻璃杯泡最好，茶叶在杯里上下起伏，非常好看。

丹　枫：好，听你的！我朋友说喝盖碗茶很多讲究，你能给我们说说吗？

静妹儿：好的，我边给你们泡茶边说。

（茶博士拿出两套汝瓷盖碗）

杜无羡：这个茶碗真好看！

静妹儿：这是汝瓷，在宋朝五大名瓷里汝瓷是最好的，以前只有皇帝才能用呢！盖碗包括茶盖、茶碗和茶船三部分。现在开始泡茶（茶博士开始泡茶，边表演边说）！泡茶分5步。首先，净具，把茶具洗一下（动作）。然后，置茶，把茶叶放进来（动作）；沏茶，把开水倒进去（动作）；闻香（动作）。你们先闻闻，再看看茶汤。茶汤绿绿的，上面的茉莉花像片片白雪，这就是为什么叫碧潭飘雪。

丹　枫：嗯，真香！

杜无羡：的确好看！

静妹儿：最后一步，品饮，可以喝了。但是，别急！（茶博士用手指在桌面叩了两下）

丹　枫：这是什么意思？

静妹儿：这是茶礼。喝茶前，你们应该对泡茶的人说谢谢。这就是谢谢。

杜无羡：哦，明白了。（两人手指叩桌子）

静妹儿：还别急，喝茶也有讲究。

（茶博士表演喝茶，左手托茶沿，右手拇指中指提起茶盖，在碗面，碗沿上轻轻拨动，发出声响，然后将茶盖半沉入水中，由里向外慢慢滑动，茶碗送到嘴边，慢慢喝，稍作停顿，发出声音分三次吞下）

这个动作叫"三吹三浪"。这样喝茶能更好地闻到茶香。

丹　枫：真不错！（享受的表情）还有其他讲究吗？

静妹儿：有的。把茶盖翻过来，放在杯沿，这是请加水的意思。把茶盖平放在碗旁，意思是这个座位上的人暂时走开，马上回来。把茶盖翻过来平放在茶碗上面，意思是"买单"。

杜无羡：真有意思！（做第一个动作）

静妹儿：好的！给您加水！

任务四

情景：何蓉蓉打电话问王成怎样才能买到好茶叶。

何蓉蓉：王成，你现在接电话方便吗？

王　成：方便！你有什么事吗！

何蓉蓉：快放假了，我想买点儿茶叶作为礼物带回国。

王　成：四川的茶很有名，买来作礼物挺好的！

何蓉蓉：那我买什么茶好呢？得向你请教请教！

王　成：竹叶青、蒙顶甘露、碧潭飘雪都是四川有名的好茶。

何蓉蓉：好的，谢谢。这些茶的名字都很好听，我先记下来。

王　成：不过，就算是同一种茶，品质也有差别。

何蓉蓉：我到底应该怎么选呢？

王　成：买茶前最好试喝一下。选茶讲究"色、香、味、形"。

何蓉蓉：哦？说来听听。

王　成：茶叶和茶汤的颜色都要好。茶叶要亮。比如，绿茶茶汤的颜色最好是淡绿色或者黄绿色。香就不用说了。茶的味道嘛，一定要鲜，说明这茶是今年的新茶。"形"就是说茶叶的大小要均匀，碎茶比较少。

何蓉蓉：太感谢了！但我还是不太懂怎么选茶，有没有简单一点的方法？

王　成：最简单的方法就是看等级。一般茶叶按品质分为特级、一级、二级等。特级最好，也最贵。你可以根据需要选合适的等级。

何蓉蓉：这个方法好！我可以放心买茶叶了。

王　成：不过，我不太建议你在网上买。买茶，和买水果差不多，尝好了再买准没错儿！

何蓉蓉：嗯！成都大街小巷茶馆多，卖茶叶的商店也不少，明天我就去买！

第九单元　快享慢活

任务一

对许多人来说，成都是一座来了就不想离开的城市。这不仅是因为成都历史悠久、文化深厚，更是因为它独特的生活方式。

成都的当代生活方式既"快"又"慢"。一方面，人们使用微信、支付宝、滴滴出行等应用程序，生活更加快捷、便利。想吃饭的时候，你可以不出门，在手机上点外卖。想看看外面世界的时候，你也可以坐在家中，通过抖音去了解……科技的发展加快了人们的生活节奏，也改变了当代中国人的生活方式。另一方面，成都人内心平和，依然喜欢安逸、舒适的慢节奏生活。人们常常去空地上跳广场舞，或者出去跑步，锻炼身体，或者去茶馆喝茶，跟朋友们聊天。天气好的时候，人们也会跟家人一起去郊区的农家乐玩儿，在郊外的田野中亲近自然，呼吸新鲜空气……

在快节奏的当代生活中，过出一种"巴适"的成都慢生活，是这个城市独特的气质与风格。

任务二

情景：王成、林一诺、杜无羡在视频聊天。

林一诺：王成，杜无羡，很高兴在微信上和你们视频通话！

王　成：杜无羡，你好啊！

杜无羡：你好，一诺。在线视频让我们聊天方便多了，距离好像也更近了。

林一诺：你们最近生活怎么样？有没有什么新鲜事儿？

王　成：上个周末我去了成都339的一家酒吧，很有意思。

林一诺：我也去过，那里人很多，玩得很开心。

杜无羡：这几天，我都没出去玩，吃饭也是点外卖。

王　成：现在不出门就能吃上好吃的，你日子过得安逸哦！

林一诺：确实。除了吃的以外，别的东西差不多也都能在网上买到。我常常在网上买书、衣服、电子产品什么的。

杜无羡：你一般在什么网站买东西？

林一诺：我喜欢在京东和淘宝上买东西。

王　成：除了买东西，我们还可以在网上看书、听音乐、看电影……甚至可以在网络上交朋友。网络大大改变了我们的生活方式。

杜无羡：对。你们玩不玩抖音？我最近爱上了看抖音。

王　成：玩啊。我也很喜欢看这个视频分享程序，在上面不仅能看到有意思的内容，还能了解多姿多彩的生活方式，但缺点是每天要占用很多时间。

林一诺：你们的生活都不错嘛。

杜无羡：现在在成都生活真是处处都离不开这些应用程序。

林一诺：我最近在研究微信和支付宝，想学习它们的商业模式，以后回国创业，开发类似的商业模式。

杜无羡：真厉害！祝你成功！

王　成：等你开发出来了，我们一起开公司吧。我出钱，你出技术。

任务三

情景：赵丽川和妈妈正要去小区广场跳广场舞，在家门口碰见何蓉蓉。

赵丽川：嗨，蓉蓉！

何蓉蓉：丽川，你好！

丽川妈妈：你好，我是丽川的妈妈。好巧，在这里碰见你。

何蓉蓉：阿姨，您好！很高兴见到您。你们现在去哪儿啊？

赵丽川：现在我俩去小区门口跳广场舞。

何蓉蓉：什么是广场舞？

赵丽川：广场舞就是很多人一起跳的舞。可以在社区广场跳，也可以在公园空地上跳，能放松心情、锻炼身体。

丽川妈妈：一般是中老年人去跳的。

何蓉蓉（问赵丽川）：那你怎么也去跳？

赵丽川：这你就不懂了吧！现在越来越多年轻人也跳广场舞了，既好玩儿，又能锻炼身体。我很多外国朋友都喜欢跳广场舞呢，他们挺喜欢这种欢快、健康的运动方式！

丽川妈妈：是啊，而且广场舞音乐中也有很多流行歌曲，跟得上潮流，年轻人也喜欢。

何蓉蓉：这样啊，真好。我也要去锻炼了，去绿道跑步！

赵丽川：咱们小区附近有绿道了？

何蓉蓉：是啊，刚建好的。每天好多人在那里跑步、散步、健身呢！你们有机会一定要去看看。

丽川妈妈：太好了，明天我就去。

赵丽川：现在我们的运动方式越来越多了，生活方式也更丰富了。好啦，我们先去跳舞了，再见！

何蓉蓉：好的，再见！

任务四

农家乐，是当代一种去乡村休闲娱乐的度假方式。城市居民来到近郊或乡村的自然环境中，放松身心，愉悦精神。

你知道吗？成都是中国农家乐的发源地。春天到了，桃花、梨花、油菜花都开了，很多成都人约着家人和朋友去附近的农家赏百花、放风筝、晒太阳、吃农家菜。夏天的时候，天气很热，人们会去山里的农家避暑、戏水、享受清凉。秋天的时候，天高气爽，瓜果飘香，市民常常周末去农家喝茶、聊天、采摘水果、买一些当地的农产品。到了冬天，大家在农家与朋友打麻将、摆龙门阵，在附近的绿道运动，忙中偷闲享受快乐的生活。美丽的田园风光、新鲜的蔬菜瓜果和安逸舒适的服务使农家乐越来越受到人们的欢迎。

第十单元　多彩中国

任务一

中国陆地面积大约960万平方公里，人口一共14亿多，有23个省、5个自治区、4个直辖市和2个特别行政区。中国面积大，人口多，各地差异也就比较大。

首先，各地的地理条件很不一样。西部有很多高原，西北部还有沙漠，中部和东部大平原比较多。

其次，各地的饮食习惯也不同。北方人喜欢吃面食，南方人喜欢吃米饭。四川、贵州和湖南等地方的人喜欢吃辣的，上海、江苏和浙江一带的人喜欢吃甜的，广东、福建这些地方的人喜欢吃清淡的。

再其次，很多地方的方言也不一样。北方方言和普通话比较像，大家差不多能互相听懂；南方很多方言差别比较大，人们互相听不懂，比如，广东人听不懂上海话，上海人也听不懂广东话。不过，虽然这些方言发音有比较大的差别，但是写的时候都用汉字。

还有，中国一共有56个民族，汉族人口最多，其他55个是少数民族。各个民族都有自己的风俗习惯和饮食特点。这56个民族团结友爱，像一个大家庭一样。

最后，中国的城市和农村也有一些差别。一般来说，城市的交通更方便，人更多，工作机会也多；农村生活压力更小，空气更新鲜，也更安静一些。城市和农村各有各的优点，所以很多人喜欢住在城市，但是也有人喜欢在农村生活。

任务二

情景：何蓉蓉、王成和赵丽川在食堂聊南北差异。

何蓉蓉：我是巴基斯坦人，你们是中国哪里人？

赵丽川：我是四川人。因为四川在中国西南，所以也算是南方人。

王　成：我是北方人，老家在山西。

何蓉蓉：在我们国家，北方和南方有很多方面不一样。中国也是这样吗？

王　成：是的，我来到成都以后，发现很多地方和我老家不一样。

何蓉蓉：你觉得中国北方和南方有什么不一样？

王　成：太多了。比如，在我老家，主食以面食为主；在四川，主食以米饭为主。

赵丽川：是的，不过在我们四川，早上也有人吃包子、馒头，中午和晚上也有人吃面条。

王　成：嗯，我老家也有人吃米饭，但是主要还是吃面食。

何蓉蓉：这样啊，我还以为中国人的主食都是米饭呢。除了吃的，还有别的什么不一样？

王　成：四川话和山西话也不太一样。我刚来成都的时候，听不太懂四川话，现在差不多能听懂了。

赵丽川：其实四川话也属于北方方言，和普通话比较接近，容易听懂，而广东话、上海话这些南方方言就没那么容易听懂了。

何蓉蓉：差别那么大，怪不得中国人都得说普通话。

赵丽川：是啊。不管说广东话还是上海话，写的时候都用汉字，所以大家还是看得懂的。

王　成：除了饮食和方言，气候也不一样。在我们老家，冬天下雪，成都冬天很少下雪，对吧？

赵丽川：没错。中国南北差异确实很大，不过我们可以到各地旅游，体验不同的文化。

任务三

情景：林一诺、何蓉蓉和乔筝在教学楼走廊聊暑假旅游经历。

林一诺：何蓉蓉、乔筝，你们暑假去旅游了吗？

何蓉蓉：去了，我们去北京旅游了。

乔　筝：我是跟何蓉蓉一起坐高铁去的。你去哪儿了？

林一诺：坐高铁很方便。我去了西昌，就是四川西南部的一个城市，离成都大概400多公里。

乔　筝：明白了，你暑假就在四川省内玩。

林一诺：是的。你们在北京玩得怎么样？

何蓉蓉：玩得非常开心！我们去了天安门广场、故宫和长城，这些地方都非常壮观，我特别喜欢。

乔　筝：我们还吃了北京烤鸭，看了一场京剧。京剧演员的衣服很漂亮。

林一诺：我也去过北京，确实非常有意思。

乔　筝：你去的西昌怎么样？

林一诺：西昌太棒了！虽然是夏天，但是不太热，听说冬天也很暖和，很舒服。

何蓉蓉：看来西昌的气候比北京的好。我们八月在北京的时候，天很热，听说北京冬天也非常冷。

林一诺：是的，西昌的气候好多了。

何蓉蓉：你去了西昌哪些地方？你觉得西昌的景点和北京的有什么不一样？

林一诺：我去了邛海，风景特别美，还去了凉山彝族博物馆。我觉得去西昌主要是看自然风景，了解当地的少数民族文化，而北京的景点大多跟历史文化有关。

乔　筝：是这样啊。那个彝族博物馆是什么？

林一诺：这个博物馆是展示彝族历史文化的地方。彝族是中国的一个少数民族，主要住在中国西南地区，西昌那边有很多彝族人。

何蓉蓉：我知道彝族。我们班有一个彝族同学，人很好，喜欢跳舞。

林一诺：你说得很对，而且西昌除了彝族以外，还有别的少数民族，比如羌族、苗族等，他们的文化都很有意思。

乔　筝：谢谢你的介绍。我很感兴趣，想明年暑假去那里看看。

何蓉蓉：西昌冬天很暖和，咱俩今年寒假就一起去。

任务四

情景：杜无羡、赵丽川在饭店和老板聊中国的城市和农村。

杜无羡：老板，你们饭店的菜真好吃！

赵丽川：就是，你们的菜还很有特色，在别的饭店一般吃不到。

钱老板：谢谢，谢谢！这是我们老家的家常菜。我是从四川农村来的，没想到老家人天天吃的菜在城里这么受欢迎。

杜无羡：我还没去过中国的农村呢。那里和城市有什么不一样？

钱老板：很多地方都不一样。比如，在农村人没有这么多，不像在成都到处都是人。

赵丽川：我有亲戚在农村，确实是这样。在农村，各家的房子一般离得比较远；在城市，大家住在楼房里，家家挨着。

钱老板：还有，农村因为人少车少，空气比城市的新鲜。

杜无羡：明白了，好像和我们国家差不多。那中国的农村有公交车吗？

赵丽川：一般没有，只有城市附近的农村才有。我觉得主要是因为农村人口比较少。

钱老板：不过由于"村村通"工程，农村的交通比以前方便多了。

赵丽川：对，现在中国正在建设美丽新农村，缩小城市和农村的差别，以后会越来越好。

杜无羡：正在建设美丽新农村啊，那我要赶快去看看。